To :

John and Maureen —

I hope you enjoy this book.
Best Regards,

Geoff G
Halfax NS
November 2018

Bounty
The Greatest
Sea Story
of Them All

Bounty
The Greatest Sea Story of Them All

GEOFF D'EON

FORMAC PUBLISHING COMPANY LIMITED
HALIFAX

Formac Publishing Company Limited recognizes the support of the Province of Nova Scotia through the Department of Communities, Culture and Heritage. We are pleased to work in partnership with the Province of Nova Scotia to develop and promote our cultural resources for all Nova Scotians. We acknowledge the support of the Canada Council for the Arts, which last year invested $153 million to bring the arts to Canadians throughout the country. This project has been made possible in part by the Government of Canada.

Cover design: Tyler Cleroux
Cover image: Alexander McClearn / Alamy Stock Photo

Library and Archives Canada Cataloguing in Publication

D'Eon, Geoff, author
    Bounty : the greatest sea story of them all / Geoff D'Eon.

Includes index.
Issued in print and electronic formats.
ISBN 978-1-4595-0544-5 (hardcover).--ISBN 978-1-4595-0554-4 (EPUB)

    1. Bounty Mutiny, 1789. 2. Bounty (Ship). 3. Ocean travel.
I. Title.

DU21.D46 2018   910.4'5   C2018-903008-9
                                              C2018-903009-7

Formac Publishing Company Limited
5502 Atlantic Street
Halifax, Nova Scotia, Canada
B3H 1G4
www.formac.ca

Printed and bound in Canada.

Contents

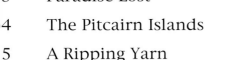

For Stuart Jolliffe
A star to steer by

Prologue

Monday, July 23, 2012, was a gorgeous summer day in Halifax, Nova Scotia. A warm breeze skimmed across the salt water, and the gentle waves were diamond studded by the afternoon sun. On the waterfront, thousands of people were gathered to wave goodbye to the twenty tall ships that for the past three days had been the city's major attraction. Tall ships festivals always draw a crowd, and this particular event was no different. There is something about the romance of sailing ships that has survived, a connection to our past, to our forefathers' essential means of transportation and the adventures they must surely have had on the high seas.

Bounty *docked at the Halifax waterfront, July 2012.*

Towering masts, billowing canvas sails and beautifully painted hulls stand in stark contrast to the modern world, and they fuel a powerful nostalgia.

One by one, the ships sailed past the waving crowds on the piers, past the red-and-white lighthouse on McNabs Island, and out toward Chebucto Head and the open ocean. There were barquentines and gaff-rigged schooners, ketches and brigs. The showboat was the magnificent USS *Eagle*, a huge, white barque, once part of Germany's navy, later a seized war trophy used to train US sailors and flamboyantly fly the Stars and Stripes.

Everywhere in the harbour, spectators bobbed in small boats, locals determined to get the best view. And there, in the middle of the procession, came the ship most photographed and — judging by the huge crowds who had walked her decks in the past three days — best loved. Not the biggest ship by any means, not sleek, but rounded. You could describe her as stout, and no one would mind.

USS Eagle *departing Halifax Harbour.*

Theodore Too *greets* Bounty.

But this was a vessel with clear attitude. Fearless, with the look of an outsider, perhaps even a pirate. This was a legendary star of the big screen. This was *Bounty*.

The spectator boats altered course to get just a little closer: sailboats from the Northwest Arm, fishing boats carrying families from Eastern Passage, a visiting megayacht carrying an anonymous millionaire — all crowded in for a better look. The children aboard the tugboat *Theodore Too* pressed closer to the rail. They could tell this ship was somehow different from the rest.

On deck, the *Bounty* crew looked lively in their distinctive green T-shirts, scurrying on deck, stowing items, belaying lines, trimming sails. They were a mixed crew of men and women, ranging in age from their early 20s to their late 60s, sun-kissed dreamers, each one with a different reason for signing on as crew, but united in their love of the ocean and their taste for adventure. Standing close to the giant, wooden ship's wheel, the grey-haired, weather-beaten captain kept a watchful eye over everything that moved.

This was not *Bounty*'s first visit to Halifax. In fact, Nova Scotia was where she was built almost fifty-two years before. She was a storied ship, an international movie star, a blue-ocean traveller. The only one of her kind in the entire world. But on this day — this gorgeous July day — she was saying goodbye to Nova Scotia forever. Just three months later, she would embark on her final, mysterious voyage. Her captain would make the most controversial decision of his long career. On a brisk fall afternoon, *Bounty* would cast off from the safety of port in Connecticut, and sail straight south into the jaws of a massive hurricane. She sustained a terrible beating. She flooded and sank just off Cape Hatteras, in the Graveyard of the Atlantic. *Bounty* took with her one of the sun-kissed dreamers, and the captain himself. Hearts were broken, inquiries were convened and a magnificent chapter of maritime history was ended.

A sailboat gets a close look at Bounty *off Point Pleasant Park.*

Bounty *leaves Halifax for the last time, July 2012.*

This is the story of two generations of *Bounty*: the original eighteenth-century British naval transport ship, on which the most infamous mutiny in British naval history played out, and also the story of her glorious twentieth-century rebirth in Lunenburg, Nova Scotia to meet the needs of a Hollywood studio. This reborn *Bounty* would sail into the twenty-first century struggling for survival.

Spanning four centuries, it is a story with all the classic ingredients: romance, risk, exotic travel, cruelty, lust, loyalty, jealousy, misadventure, hubris, heroism and death. A story with timeless lessons for us all.

CHAPTER 1
Voyage to Paradise

If it weren't for *Artocarpus altilis* — better known as breadfruit — the *Bounty* story might never have happened. Breadfruit is a species of flowering tree in the mulberry and fig family. It produces large quantities of an edible fruit the size of a person's head. Most North Americans and Europeans have never seen it, let alone tasted it. But these days it is commonplace in many parts of Asia, the Pacific islands, Central America and the Caribbean.

Two hundred and fifty years ago, in 1769, a wealthy British botanist named Sir Joseph Banks came across breadfruit in Tahiti, while on an expedition with the famous explorer Captain James Cook. Banks was quite taken with the discovery. Breadfruit trees need little to no maintenance and grow readily in a tropical climate. The

Breadfruit are very rich in starch and are a staple food in many tropical regions.

Portrait of Joseph Banks by Joshua Reynolds (1773).

tree exudes a latex that the Tahitians used as glue and caulking. The wood from the tree was used to build canoes. But to Banks, the botanist and opportunist, by far the most intriguing thing about breadfruit was its utility as a staple food product. When boiled or roasted, breadfruit is akin to potatoes or yams. Some people said it tasted like bread, and that was that.

In the late eighteenth century, Great Britain was heavily invested in the slave trade, with captured Africans being forced to work on sugar plantations in the Caribbean. While people were enslaved by the usual brutal methods, the means to sustain them was not readily available. Inconveniently for the masters, slaves had to be fed if they were to have strength to work. Encouraged and entreated by plantation owners in Jamaica, Banks became deeply involved in what was seen as a brilliant solution: breadfruit seedlings must be gathered in Tahiti and transplanted to the Caribbean.

Banks was a man of science, much celebrated on his safe return to England in 1771 for having collected an unprecedented number of exotic plant species. This was an age when there existed great passion for geographic discovery, exploration and the acquisition of scientific knowledge. Banks — with his brilliant mind and considerable fortune — was a beacon. He went on to become the president of

Top: Royal Navy ships at Deptford.
Painting by John Cleveley the Elder (1754).
Right: *Map of the Caribbean from 1715.*

the Royal Society and founded what became the pre-eminent botanical garden in the world, Kew Gardens near London. In his day, Banks was a hugely influential power-broker, every bit as famous as Steve Jobs or Bill Gates are today. As the years passed, Banks would not let go of the notion to source cheap food for the slave trade. In part, this was because Banks had financial interests in the plantation business. He put up a cash prize — a 'bounty' — for anyone who could make the scheme workable. Eventually, in 1787 he was successful in persuading the British Navy to launch an expedition to gather breadfruit seedlings in Tahiti and to transport them to the West Indies.

This was no small undertaking, yet it wouldn't have been considered a glamorous assignment for whatever ship, crew or captain that could be found to do the job. At the time, the British Navy had more pressing matters at hand than procuring a lumpy green fruit that few people in England had ever heard of. There were endless wars to be fought with the French, the Dutch and the Spanish for dominion over the world's oceans and for the spoils of colonization.

The American colonies were seized with insurrection and independence. In France, the seeds of an impending revolution were taking root. The British Navy's focus was on commissioning and building large, heavily armed fighting ships. Britain was a superpower to be defended. What on earth would the King's Navy use for a glorified gardening expedition, literally on the other side of the world? Who in heaven would want to command . . . a floating greenhouse?

When he first laid eyes on the ship that would become *Bounty*, William Bligh was thirty-three years old. He was married with four children. Times were hard. His once-bright naval career had stalled since the end of the American War of Independence. Demand for naval officers had declined and Bligh had found work as a captain on merchant ships, carrying rum and sugar from the West Indies. He was an experienced mariner and a brilliant navigator. Bligh's claim to fame was that in his younger days he had been chosen by Captain James Cook as sailing master on Cook's third and final expedition to the Pacific.

Oil painting of Sir Joseph Banks (seated) with Captain James Cook and others by John Hamilton Mortimer (1771).

Bligh was there when Cook was killed in a violent skirmish with natives, and he was proud to have served with such a British hero. Now, in need of respectable work, he stared hard at the lumpy vessel offered to him by the Royal Navy.

The ship was no beauty. She was originally built in northern England as a "merchantman," potentially a coal carrier. She measured ninety feet long on deck. She was a three-masted workhorse of the sea, a sturdy little 215-ton ship, but not quite what an ambitious navy captain might want on a new

Portrait of William Bligh by John Webber (1776).

assignment that would take him to the other side of world. At her launch, she had been christened *Bethia.* Seeing her potential for the task at hand, the Royal Navy purchased her for the modest sum of £1,950 and went about converting her as required. As Bligh weighed the pros and cons of taking command, he could not have been an entirely happy man.

The Royal Navy commissioned her on August 16, 1787. She was designated "His Majesty's Armed Vessel *Bounty*" (HMAV), rather than "His Majesty's Ship (HMS) *Bounty.*" Armed vessel was a bit of a stretch: *Bounty* had just four four-pound canons and ten half-pounder swivel guns, miserably small firepower for a vessel about to circumnavigate the globe in turbulent times. Below deck, her interior had been customized to maximize her ability to carry seedlings. Sir Joseph Banks was a key designer of the ship's modifications. The best space of all — the "grand cabin" in the stern of the ship, the one

Flogging on board a British Navy ship, with the crew assembled to witness the punishment. Engraving by George Cruickshank (1825).

with the instantly recognizable square-pane windows looking aft, the space almost always reserved for the captain in which to work — had been equipped with shelving to accommodate 600 plants.

Bligh himself was assigned a windowless, eight-by-seven feet cabin. To add insult to injury, the Royal Navy declined to officially designate Bligh as a captain for this expedition. Rather, they offered him the job at his previous rank: a lieutenant. Not only was this a blow to Bligh's pride, but it would hurt his pocketbook, too. At the same time, the expedition itself would save money. Finally, in ways that no one could have predicted, the lesser rank of lieutenant would resound in the months ahead, when ship's discipline would be at a premium. Multiple entreaties fell on deaf ears. Sir Joseph Banks himself, who had personally recommended Bligh for this expedition, was unable to help. So, while as the ranking officer on the ship he might be called "Captain Bligh," he remained a lieutenant.

Eighteenth-century caricature of a press gang at work.

Resigned to his situation and with an eye to future promotion, Bligh set his mind to assembling his crew.

It was a mixed bunch who reported for duty. Life in the service of His Majesty's eighteenth-century Navy was no picnic. There was no such thing as sanitation, privacy or a good night's sleep on a ship. The food was bad, the work was hard, and the discipline could be unsparing. Floggings were the order of the day on a regular basis. Fear was used as a weapon. Disease — including scurvy, dysentery and "venereals" — was ever-present. Dr. Johnson famously remarked that going to sea was akin to going to prison, with the added danger of drowning.

Still, especially for gentlemen destined for the officer class, serving in the navy was a respectable living. Those who chose a naval career started young, and it was commonplace for boys as young as twelve to go to sea. The navy attracted the uneducated, the working class, the poor and the hard-bitten. Sometimes at dockside, roving press gangs simply beat men senseless and forced them on board. To succeed as able seamen, men became skilled, courageous and resourceful. Commanding the respect of such men was not easily done. This was the job of the officers, and the safety of the ship and everyone aboard depended on them doing it well.

The *Bounty* complement included forty-three navy personnel, two civilian botanists and one single commissioned officer: William Bligh. In those days, a squad of armed marines was often added to a ship's complement, to protect the ship and officers, to enforce order at sea and to act as a security team when ashore. *Bounty* was too small to accommodate marines, so she had none. She did have a cooper (barrelmaker) to build and maintain special shelving and

Engraving of Admiralty House in London by Robert Sands (1831).

planters, a surgeon, a cook, a butcher, a gunner and a carpenter, in addition to a dozen able seamen and six midshipmen (naval officers-in-training). All were Englishmen, but the sailmaker — one Lawrence LeBogue — hailed from Nova Scotia. LeBogue had signed on to the First Fleet, the convoy of ships assigned that very same year to settle the penal colony that would later become Australia. Records indicate that LeBogue quit that expedition before it left Plymouth and, soon after, joined *Bounty*'s crew. The master, who was responsible for the day-to-day operation of the ship and who reported directly to Bligh, was John Fryer. There were two master's mates, one of whom was to become the epicentre of the *Bounty* story: Fletcher Christian.

Christian — according to Bligh's description — was "dark and very swarthy" and slightly bow-legged. He first went to sea at the relatively late age of eighteen. Christian's father died when he was just a boy, and though initially well-to-do, the family had run into financial hardship. They hoped that young Fletcher would be their salvation. With time and opportunities running out, Fletcher Christian took the last best option available to him: naval service. On two previous expeditions he had sailed under Bligh and had become a protegé of his, learning the skills required at sea. Christian and Bligh respected each other, and it was Bligh who recommended to the Admiralty that Christian be assigned as master's mate on HMAV *Bounty*. Essentially, Bligh did Christian a favour and got him a job. Bligh had no sons, only daughters, and in time Bligh became a mentor to his younger shipmate. Christian visited Bligh's home between voyages, and their relationship was cordial. Both men would have known what to expect from the other as they watched the *Bounty*'s crew assemble for inspection. Christian was not alone in having sailed with Lieutenant William Bligh before. Three of the men had been with Bligh on Captain Cook's last voyage to the Pacific. They knew the challenges and dangers that lay ahead. To fill the

British Warship Leaving Portsmouth Harbour *by John Cleveley the Younger (1773).*

positions, Bligh also recruited individuals he had worked with when he commanded merchant ships.

These forty-five crewmen settled in, stowed the provisions and their few possessions and made final preparations for departure. Eight hundred clay pots were loaded, along with food, muskets, ammunition, drawing supplies, fresh water, rum and glass beads as "trinkets for the natives." Every conceivable space was used. The former merchantman had been completely refitted and was now stuffed to the gills with everything that might be needed on a journey estimated to last more than a year. On deck lay *Bounty's* three small boats. One of them had been especially ordered to size by Bligh, a twenty-three-foot-long launch, a bigger boat than would usually be carried. Unbeknownst to anyone as *Bounty* slipped her lines in London and headed for Portsmouth, this same unassuming launch would soon be put to the test in one of the greatest open-boat voyages in maritime history.

> *The men are all in excellent spirits, and I have still the greatest confidence of success in every part of the voyage.*
> — *William Bligh's log entry on departure*

Things got off to a bad start. With *Bounty* anchored off Portsmouth, Bligh was instructed to wait for official permission to depart. The Admiralty had strict control of the comings and goings of naval vessels. Bligh became furious as the days went by and favourable sailing conditions came and went. His plan was to sail for Cape Horn on the southern tip of South America, and from there west into the Pacific. But he had to do it soon, before winter set in and rounding the Horn became impossible. The Admiralty was focused on the possibility of a fresh war with Holland and ignored Bligh's increasingly urgent requests. Weeks went by without sailing orders being received. Bligh was beside himself, writing furious letters to colleagues on shore. Eventually, the "breadfruit expedition" was given the go-ahead. *Bounty* weighed anchor and proceeded to sail smack into headwinds that further delayed her by three weeks. It was December 23, 1787, before *Bounty's* journey to Tahiti got properly underway. Bligh was running late, and as they headed for Cape Horn and the world's most dangerous waters, everyone on board knew by the time *Bounty* reached Cape Horn, the winter storms had set in. The headwinds and storms *Bounty* faced were terrifying in their force. For a full month, *Bounty* and her crew were lashed by gales, making little headway. Bligh recorded in his log that "the storm exceeded anything I had met

British Royal Navy ships visiting Matavai Bay, Tahiti. Painting by John Cleveley the Younger (1787).

a large, sheltered bay, in the shadows of forest-covered volcanoes. Immediately, canoes headed out from shore to greet the square-rigger. This was a collision of two very different worlds. The English sailors — skinny, pockmarked and (except for the youngest of them) mostly toothless — saw for the first time what the inhabitants of this island paradise looked like. The Tahitians were gorgeous, the men and the women. The *Bounty* sailors would have heard the stories about the "friendlies," and now they were seeing for themselves. Bligh and some of the others who had been here years before with Cook were welcomed back. The entire crew was regaled with gifts of flowers and fresh fruit as the islanders climbed aboard and swarmed over *Bounty*'s decks. The uninhibited sexual flirting of the Tahitian women was something eighteenth-century Englishmen had never encountered before, even in their wildest dreams. For some of them, the prospect of exotic encounters was the very reason they tolerated the brutality of naval service.

> *It was the finest island in the world, where the inhabitants need not labour, and where the allurements of dissipation are beyond anything that can be conceived.*
>
> — *Captain William Bligh*

With each kiss, with each flowered garland placed around the sailors' necks, with every sip of fresh sweet water, a new world of infinite and joyous possibilities was opening up. The long-suffering and battered crew — having managed to bring *Bounty* halfway around the world to this island paradise — sensed it was time for their reward. There would be no stopping them.

CHAPTER 2
Garden of Eden

Tahiti is certainly the paradise of the world, and if happiness could result from situation and convenience here it is to be found in the highest perfection. I have seen many parts of the world but Tahiti is capable of being preferable to them all.

— CAPTAIN WILLIAM BLIGH, LOGBOOK ENTRY

It's hard to underestimate the culture shock experienced by the *Bounty*'s crew as they settled into island life. The paradise they found themselves in would have been nothing at all like eighteenth-century Europe. Where England could be cold and damp, Tahiti was

Tahitians greet the arrival of Bounty, *as depicted by MGM in 1962.*

caressed by warm offshore breezes and bathed in sunshine. While England's typical diet would have been poor for most of the men, here they feasted daily on fresh fruit and roasted meats. While life aboard ship was a daily grind of rigorous physical toil, here the days were relaxed, and the living was easy. Too easy, in the eyes of William Bligh. He watched as his crew intermingled with the Tahitians. To Bligh's dismay, he saw attachments being formed, romantic and sexual relationships blossoming. It was a disciplinarian's nightmare.

Collecting the breadfruit seedlings began in late October. But it was clear there would be a delay in *Bounty*'s eventual departure, since the plants had to be sufficiently mature to endure transportation. None of *Bounty*'s crew were in any kind of hurry. The weeks drifted by in their new-found Garden of Eden. Slowly but surely, hundreds of seedlings were collected and tended to in the onshore nursery. Bligh regularly entertained the native chiefs and their attendants aboard *Bounty*, as diplomacy dictated. Meanwhile on shore, several of the crew underwent the Tahitian's painful custom of tattooing, with special attention paid to adorning the buttocks. No one seemed to embrace the Tahitian way of life more enthusiastically than Fletcher Christian. He became inseparable from Maimiti, the tall, beautiful daughter of one of the chiefs. Diagnosed cases of venereal disease among the crew increased; Christian was one of them.

The seasons changed, and around Christmas the rains set in. *Bounty*'s doctor — by all accounts a dissolute and hopeless drunkard — keeled over and died. There were several instances of insubordination from the crew that resulted in floggings. In early January, three of the sailors deserted, and had to be hunted down with the help of the Tahitians and returned to the ship. The men were punished with the lash, but not to the extent naval law allowed for desertion. Bligh was trying to strike a delicate balance, attempting to maintain the loyalty of the crew while ensuring a semblance of order. He must have known his grip on the situation was precarious at best.

In all, it would take five months before *Bounty* could be finally loaded with her precious breadfruit cargo. There was a palpable sense of dread as the day of departure came closer. Strong bonds between many of the ship's company and the islanders had been forged, not to mention romances and pregnancies. Bligh remained steadfastly focused on the job at hand. For all his faults — his quick temper, his furious outbursts and insults, his rigid adherence to British standards of behaviour — he was undeniably a consummate

The distinctive jagged peaks of Tahiti.

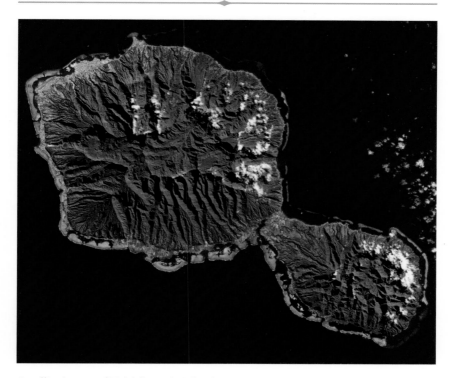

Satellite image of Tahiti's main island.

naval professional. Very soon, this single-mindedness would prove to be a liability.

The wailing and weeping of the distraught Tahitians as *Bounty* weighed anchor on April 5, 1789, would not have softened Bligh's resolve. Successful completion of his mission held the promise of a promotion to full captain's status. All other trivial concerns — including the emotional state of his crew — were swept aside. As he ordered the sails set to begin the long voyage to the West Indies, Bligh was in no mind to tolerate the least resistance.

CHAPTER 3
Paradise Lost

The first week of April 1789, *Bounty* set a course westward from Tahiti. The southern trade winds were favourable, and progress was good. *Bounty*'s food lockers were well stocked. The nights were clear, and Bligh used his expertise in celestial navigation to keep *Bounty* steadily on course for New Holland (now Australia). But while all outward signs indicated business as usual, a toxic brew of discontent had begun to ferment below decks.

Bounty *at sea.*

There are several different accounts of *Bounty*'s journey from Tahiti: Bligh's, of course; but also accounts from the malcontent Bosun's Mate James Morrison (written years later), the Master John Fryer's, and even one related by the Nova Scotian sailmaker Lawrence LeBogue. In subsequent years, many of the crew members would be called upon to tell their story. The details differ in many respects. Each account was probably composed to show the writer in the best possible light.

After three weeks of good sailing, *Bounty* arrived in Tonga. Bligh had visited these islands eleven years before with Captain Cook. The natives here were notably less hospitable than the Tahitians. Tonga was a paradise in which European visitors were in constant danger. The shore party was threatened as they gathered fresh water and wood. Following one particularly tense encounter with natives, Bligh publicly accused Fletcher Christian of cowardice. This would have been seen by all on board *Bounty* as a serious insult. Things were to get much worse shortly after. *Bounty* was again under sail, making course west toward the tip of New Holland and the island of New Guinea. Many of the crew were now unhappy. They grieved for their lost life of luxury and lovemaking back in Tahiti. Seemingly oblivious, Bligh became more abusive than usual, insulting the officers with mounting frequency, for the smallest of infractions. Stung by verbal assaults, Christian began to decline Bligh's usual invitation to dine with him. Morale on *Bounty* was unravelling.

In the end, it all came down to coconuts.

Bounty was well supplied with coconuts. Each man and officer had an allowance. Coconuts kept well on board, and were a ready source of vitamins, fibre, minerals and sweet liquid. The nuts were piled on deck between the guns. On the morning of April 27, 1789, Captain Bligh awoke and while walking on deck, imagined that the coconut pile had shrunk overnight. He proceeded to interrogate each of the officers. How many nuts had they purchased on shore? How many had they eaten? How many had they now? When it was

Christian's turn, the situation went from bad to worse. Christian, trying to maintain his composure, protested to Bligh that the captain couldn't possibly think Christian had stolen something as trivial as a coconut? Bligh — his fury unabated — thundered back that indeed he did think it possible. For Christian — first accused of cowardice and now of theft — it was all too much to bear. Forced by duty to abandon his love Maimiti, now more than a thousand nautical miles behind him on Tahiti, Christian was in torment. A combination of grief, humiliation and anger overwhelmed Christian. Literally in tears, he arrived at a momentous and irreversible decision.

At dawn on April 28, Captain William Bligh woke up with a violent start. Fletcher Christian and three other men, armed with pistols and cutlasses, seized the captain, rolled him over and tied his hands behind his back. Within minutes, naked under his nightshirt, Bligh was forced on deck. There, he came face to face with the dangerous chaos of an unfolding and full-blown mutiny.

That morning on *Bounty*'s decks, there were hours of angry shouting, arguing, pleading, and threats of violence. Christian had taken charge of the ship and had the support of eighteen crew members. With emotions running at fever pitch, they pointed weapons and hurled insults at Bligh and the officers and men loyal to him. Some of the crew, realizing the enormity of the crime unfolding before them, kept silent. In fact, the men opposed to the illegal seizing of the ship outnumbered the mutineers. No matter. The mutineers had the initiative and the weapons. Bligh's original misgivings about not having marines on board to protect the ship were now fully vindicated. Some of the mutineers wanted Bligh killed on the spot. Bligh held his ground, loudly protesting the outrage being perpetrated. Christian bellowed back "Not another word sir, or you are dead!" Bligh challenged Christian to do it — to kill him right then and there. Christian would not. For all his mental anguish and torment, he was not a murderer.

At last, Christian announced his decision: Bligh and those loyal to him would be put over the side into the *Bounty*'s largest launch, the one Bligh had especially ordered before departure. It was twenty-three feet long, and less than six feet wide. It was now loaded to the gunnels with eighteen men, including the disgraced Master Fryer, the gunner, the carpenter, half of the midshipmen, the quartermasters, and the Nova Scotian sailmaker Lawrence LeBogue. They were provided with some bread, pork and rum, and twenty-eight gallons of drinking water. Given their location, the horribly overloaded boat, and its meagre supplies, this was in effect a slow death sentence. Four additional men loyal to Bligh couldn't fit onto the launch and were obliged to stay aboard *Bounty*. Murderous threats were in the air. Confusion and fear choked in the men's throats.

Captain Bligh and his followers set adrift. Painting by Robert Dodd (1790).

Bligh never broke and kept his dignity intact as he made one last desperate appeal: "Consider, Mr. Christian. I have a wife and four children in England, you have danced my children upon your knee."

At the point of a bayonet, Bligh was forced over the side and into the launch. "I am in hell. I am in hell!" Christian shouted, on the verge of hysteria.

Accompanied by jeers and insults from the mutineers, the launch was let go, and pushed away from the safety of *Bounty,* into the endless blue Pacific. Within hours, it would be a poor tiny speck on the vastness of the ocean. The mutiny on the *Bounty* was now a fact. The extraordinary events that followed secured its place in the annals of maritime history.

Fletcher Christian needed a plan. There was no more serious crime in the navy than mutiny. It carried the death penalty, and for the rest of their lives Christian and his accomplices would be fugitives. The other certainty was that eventually the British Navy would come looking for them. Improvising his strategy, Christian turned *Bounty* around, and set a course back the way they had just come, toward to the island of Tubuai, south of Tahiti. Ironically, it was thanks to Bligh that Tubuai was as well-known as it was. The small island had been charted years before by Bligh himself, during one of Cook's expeditions. Tubuai proved not to be the sanctuary Christian might have hoped. Soon after arrival, hostilities broke out between Christian's crew and the islanders, fights most often about provisions, or taking Indigenous women as "wives." After two months of failed negotiation and fighting, Christian decided to return *Bounty* to Tahiti. There, sixteen of the crew elected to stay permanently, including the four crewmen loyal to Bligh not able to fit into the *Bounty*'s launch. The Bligh loyalists calculated that when eventually discovered by the navy, they would be able to plead their case, and disavow the mutiny.

At about the same time, thousands of nautical miles to the west, Bligh and the eighteen others in *Bounty*'s overloaded launch

Tahiti: for Bounty's *mutineers, a paradise lost.*

long ago — their beautiful Garden of Eden, where warm offshore breezes gently caress endless yellow and red flowers, and turquoise water laps the sand.

Captain William Bligh meanwhile was back at sea. He had been entrusted with another Royal Navy ship, HMS *Providence*, and had been assigned to return to Tahiti in a second attempt to gather breadfruit seedlings. This time the mission was accomplished. Four months after the hanging of the *Bounty* mutineers, Bligh landed his breadfruit plants in Jamaica. But after a saga that had gone on for years, a terrible irony now set in. The slaves on the sugar plantations disliked the breadfruit so much they refused to eat it. Bligh's precious cargo, achieved at such high cost, was fed to the island's pigs.

CHAPTER 4
The Pitcairn Islands

The Pitcairn Islands, situated at latitude 24.38° south, longitude 128.32° west, are tiny bursts of volcanic basalt rock poking through the surface of the South Pacific Ocean, midway between New Zealand and South America.

Whatever resemblance to paradise Pitcairn represented for Fletcher Christian and the other *Bounty* fugitives in January 1790, it was short-lived. After HMAV *Bounty* was set on fire and sunk, the group went about the business of becoming settlers. They built small houses, they fished, they grew crops, and even fashioned a rudimentary still to make alcohol. In time, they began having

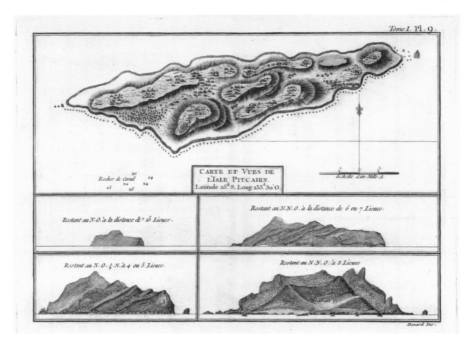

Map and elevations of Pitcairn by Robert Bernard (1774).

Portrait of John Adams, one of the Bounty *mutineers.*

children. Petty resentments and bitter jealousies — especially regarding the women — became magnified. Squabbles became fights, fuelled by alcohol. Fights became murders. Christian himself is said to have descended into a deeply troubled malaise. The *Bounty* mutineers took to mistreating the Tahitian men, and the Tahitians would have none of it. Deadly fights broke out. In one version of the story (there are several accounts, and they conflict) Christian is said to have been shot and killed. By the time the multiple conflicts were over, all the Tahitian men were dead. All but two of the original *Bounty* men were murdered.

By 1799, nine years after their arrival, the Pitcairn settlement consisted of just two mutineers, the Tahitian women, and numerous

John Adams's house on Pitcairn. Etching by Robert Batty (1831).

children born from the various unions. On Christmas Day 1800, former Bounty Midshipman Ned Young died from complications related to asthma. That left just one single surviving mutineer.

As the years slipped by, no passing ships landed on Pitcairn. It wasn't until 1808 that an American whaling ship came close in. The Americans on board were astonished to see smoke rising from a settlement on what was well-known to be an uninhabited island. To their amazement, among a group of middle-aged Tahitian women, they encountered a wild-haired man who spoke fluent English. He claimed to *be* English and claimed to know Royal Navy Captain William Bligh. He was former Able Seaman John Adams — now going by the name Alexander Smith — the sole survivor of the mutiny on the *Bounty* almost twenty years earlier.

Among the excited Pitcairn Islanders staring hard at the American strangers was a tall, handsome man in his early twenties named after the day he was born: Thursday October Christian, the

*Portrait of Thursday October Christian by John
Schillibeer (1814).*

island's first-born resident, the oldest son of Fletcher Christian. He
had a younger brother Charles, and a still younger sister Mary Ann.

It is largely from Adams's accounts that we know what
happened to the *Bounty* mutineers, although it is said that
Adams's versions of events varied depending who he was telling,
and when. And of course, the Tahitian women had accounts of
their own to share. Whatever tales are believed, Christian's dream
of living out his days in a tropical idyll was dashed to pieces. It
was an epic failure.

Today, Pitcairn Islands is Britain's smallest colony, administered from an office in New Zealand. Some fifty people live there, clustered around the aptly named capital Adamstown. It is inhabited predominantly by the descendants of Fletcher Christian's original colonists.

It is still a remote place, not much visited, with an aging and shrinking population. In recent years, Pitcairn offered free land to anyone willing to relocate there. There was one single applicant.

Bounty scholars and enthusiasts have made repeated visits, seeking to flesh out the details of the *Bounty* saga. In 1933, the remnants of *Bounty*'s wooden rudder were spotted by one Parkin Christian. A subsequent 1957 diving expedition in Bounty Bay recovered parts of the rudder, the anchor and other artifacts from the wreck.

Bounty's original anchor, recovered from the wreck in 1957; displayed today outside the town hall in Adamstown.

A model of HMAV Bounty *burns on Bounty Day, the community's annual commemoration of the original ship's destruction on January 23, 1790.*

Another archaeological expedition mounted in 1998 recovered many items — both from the wreck and on land: nails, cannonballs, grapeshot, clay pipe fragments, small bottles and broken ceramics. Today, what is left of HMAV *Bounty's* rudder is preserved and displayed in a museum on the distant island of Fiji.

Every January, in a ritualistic nod to their ancestry, Pitcairn Islanders meet by the rocks and gather around a wooden model of *Bounty*. There, the model is set on fire and the islanders watch as it burns — a small but significant way the *Bounty* story has continued into the twenty-first century.

Nearby, John Adams's gravesite is well marked, along with the graves of some of the other early settlers. Adams survived as patriarch on Pitcairn for thirty-nine years, and was granted amnesty, the British Navy being occupied with more pressing matters, including the Napoleonic Wars. Adams eventually died in 1829, the last of *Bounty's* mutineers.

The grave of John Adams, Pitcairn Island.

Fletcher Christian's death remains shrouded in mystery. Was he murdered? Was he driven to madness? Did he commit suicide? One theory has it that he escaped Pitcairn and lived out his days in anonymity back in England. Whatever his fate, his lineal descendants can still be traced. In an extraordinary twist of fate, one of these descendants would find herself fighting for her life in another ship named *Bounty*, in another time, on another ocean, six generations away.

Parkin Christian, a direct descendant of Fletcher Christian, on Pitcairn, 1935.

CHAPTER 5
A Ripping Yarn

Now don't mistake me. I'm not advising cruelty or brutality with no purpose. My point is that cruelty with purpose is not cruelty — it's efficiency. Then a man will never disobey once he's watched his mate's backbone laid bare. He'll see the flesh jump, hear the whistle of the whip for the rest of his life.
　　　　— CAPTAIN BLIGH, AS PORTRAYED BY TREVOR HOWARD
　　　　　　　(IN MGM'S 1962 *MUTINY ON THE BOUNTY*)

Never let the facts get in the way of a good story.
　　　　　　　— ENTERTAINMENT INDUSTRY MAXIM

Trevor Howard as Captain William Bligh, 1962.

From the day William Bligh returned to England in March 1790, word started to spread. The newspapers of the day churned the story out, and readers ate it up. Bligh had, through raw courage and navigational genius, saved the lives of eighteen of *Bounty*'s loyal crew. The word "hero" was bandied about. Once the Admiralty's court martial found him blameless for the mutiny, the die appeared to be cast: the brave Lieutenant Bligh was to be admired and promoted; the coward Christian Fletcher was to be reviled and brought to justice. Life is rarely this simple, and it proved not to be in this case either. Through political manoeuvring and self-serving revisionist storytelling, the saga of the mutiny on the *Bounty* underwent a dramatic metamorphosis.

Driven by the need to exonerate himself more completely, Bligh published his own account, grandly entitled *A Narrative of the Mutiny, on Board His Majesty's Ship* Bounty; *and the Subsequent Voyage of Part of the Crew, in the Ship's Boat, from Tofoa, one of the Friendly Islands, to Timor, a Dutch Settlement in the East Indies.* Following this, Bligh was appointed captain of a new vessel, much larger, better armed, and with a complement of marines for protection. He sailed back to Tahiti, in the second — and successful — attempt to gather breadfruit seedlings.

It was during his absence that the trial of the recaptured mutineers took place. The malcontent Bosun's Mate James Morrison penned his own memorandum, which was distributed to the twelve navy judges. With his life on the line, Morrison sought an acquittal by portraying William Bligh as a tyrant, unfit to command in the King's Navy. Another of the accused, young Peter Heywood, enjoyed family connections with one of the judges. Quiet lobbying behind the scenes began, with the principal strategy being to blame Bligh for the mutiny. It paid off. Both men were pardoned after being found guilty. At the same time, Fletcher Christian's older brother Edward began the work of restoring the family's reputation. Edward Christian was a law professor at Cambridge, and his prospects for advancement

HMAV Bounty *midshipman Peter Heywood.*

were stymied by association with the infamous mutiny. Edward
convened a panel of "distinguished gentlemen" to hear first-hand
the stories of the surviving *Bounty* crew. Unsurprisingly, much of the
panel's recorded testimony supported the contention that Fletcher
Christian was a man of upstanding virtue. The eventual publication
of Edward Christian's report — eagerly consumed by followers of
the *Bounty* story — was a serious blow to William Bligh's reputation.
By the time Bligh returned from the second breadfruit expedition,
his hero status had evaporated. Adding to Bligh's problems, James
Morrison's damning "memorandum" was complete but — for the
time being — unpublished.

Morrison died in 1808, leaving his memoir with his *Bounty*
shipmate Peter Heywood. It remained hidden for twenty-three
years, until it was uncovered by distinguished British author and
statesman Sir John Barrow. In 1831, Barrow wrote a bestseller:
The Eventful History of the Mutiny and Piratical Seizure of HMS

Bounty. As source material, Barrow drew liberally from Morrison's self-serving and uncontested memoir, adding to Bligh's growing notoriety as a brutish tyrant.

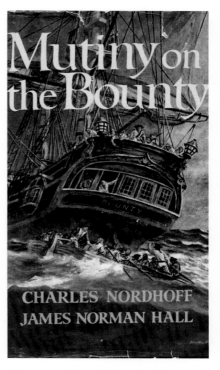

The first-known cinematic treatment of the *Bounty* story was an Australian–New Zealand silent film made in 1916, *The Mutiny of the Bounty*. The poster boasts it consists of "five reels," which presumably would have impressed an audience in those early days of moving pictures. Since the film was largely based on Bligh's own journals, he was not depicted as the ogre he was destined to become. The film was the most expensive Australian movie made to date. Tahitians were played by a Maori cast, and characters included the breadfruit expedition's initiator Sir Joseph Banks, as well as King George III.

The cover of Nordoff and Hall's 1932 bestseller.

By all accounts, the film was a hit with audiences. However, few prints were made, and none are known to have survived. Sadly, this is considered a "lost film."

Fast-forward fifteen years to 1931. The American writers Charles Nordoff and James Norman Hall had begun their three-part, fictionalized account of the *Bounty* story — based in part on Sir John Barrow's century-old book. From beyond the grave, *Bounty* Bosun's Mate James Morrison was wreaking his revenge on Captain Bligh.

Nordoff and Hall's 1932 novel *Mutiny on the Bounty* was a bestseller, as were the two related books that followed. Their Bligh-as-villain version became the basis for later film adaptations. The first of them was a 1933 Australian movie *In the Wake of Bounty*, a peculiar, low-budget, drama-travelogue, featuring a long-forgotten cast. There was one exception. The part of Fletcher Christian was played by an as-yet unknown, dashing newcomer who would go on to become a screen legend: Errol Flynn.

This relatively obscure film treatment was quickly followed by Metro-Goldwyn-Mayer's (MGM) much more substantial 1935 offering *Mutiny on the Bounty*.

It was in this film that the caricature of the tyrannical Captain Bligh was established once and for all. In the role of a lifetime, Charles Laughton's splenetic performance of Bligh as a half-mad,

Top: *Charles Laughton depicts MGM's sadistic and tyrannical Captain Bligh, 1935.*

Right: *Screen idol Clark Gable as Fletcher Christian, with co-star Mamo Clark.*

Original 1935 poster for MGM's Mutiny on the Bounty.

sadistic villain resonated with audiences all over the world. The part of the sympathetic and sensitive Fletcher Christian was again played by a handsome American movie idol. This time, it was heartthrob Clark Gable.

Critics raved about the production. The *New York Times* gushed: "Grim, brutal, sturdily romantic, made out of horror and desperate courage, it is as savagely exciting and rousingly dramatic a photoplay as has come out of Hollywood in recent years." The Academy of Motion Pictures agreed, and *Mutiny on the Bounty* won the 1935 Oscar for Best Picture. The name Bligh became synonymous with brutality and remains so to this day.

Twenty-five years later, MGM's fortunes were in decline, and the studio desperately needed a hit. The epic remake of *Ben Hur* in 1959 had succeeded at the box office, and the studio executives gambled they had another winner when they decided to remake the *Mutiny on the Bounty*. No expense would be spared. This new version would be shot on location in Tahiti and would be filmed using the latest technology: Ultra Panavision Widescreen. It would be presented with cutting-edge projectors, and four-track "surround sound" effects. MGM's plan was to dazzle audiences with the highest possible production values. A stellar cast was assembled. Fletcher Christian would be played by superstar Marlon Brando — famous for his Oscar win for *On the Waterfront*. Captain Bligh would be played by veteran British character actor Trevor Howard. MGM wanted to see their newest Bligh portrayed as a sneering Englishman with a sharp tongue, a quick temper, and a nasty streak of sadism. Trevor Howard was their man. Charles Laughton's brutish portrayal had worked box office magic in 1935. Why change a winning formula?

MGM had one last trick up its sleeve. They needed a ship to represent HMAV *Bounty*. Previous films had used look-alikes. But in keeping with the spare-no-expense approach to this new would-be blockbuster, MGM made a bold decision. They would build an exact replica of the original *Bounty*, based on the original designs that were still in safekeeping in the UK. This was to be no mere movie prop. This was to be a fully rigged ocean-going ship, capable of getting herself to the location in Tahiti. She had to be fitted with ten thousand square feet of sails, all the rigging plus accurate eighteenth-century-style fittings. Of course, she would be equipped with diesel engines too. Verisimilitude has its limits, and there would be shooting schedules to keep. Building an actual full-scale wooden ship had never been attempted before by a motion picture studio. The idea was a publicist's dream.

The next and most obvious question: where could such a project be undertaken? Where on the planet could MGM find shipbuilders who knew the old ways? Who could lift an eighteenth-century plan from fading parchment, and work a modern miracle with wood, iron, rope and canvas? A tender was issued. Bids came in from boatyards in the United States, Europe, even one from Japan. But among them, there was a clear winner, a natural choice: Lunenburg, Nova Scotia.

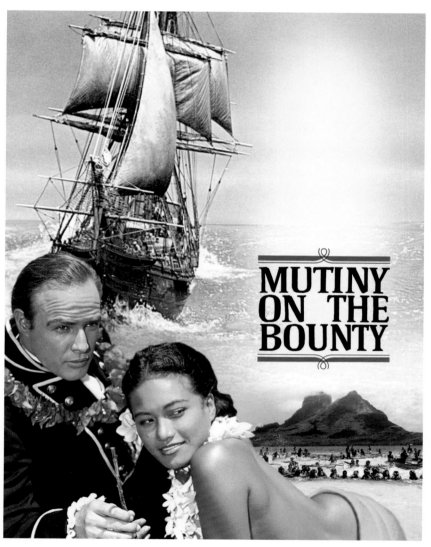

MGM made the bold decision to build a replica of the original Bounty *for its 1962 epic and featured the ship prominently in its marketing materials.*

CHAPTER 6
Bounty Reborn

When the Bounty *is finally shipshape, wherever she sails with her will go the reputation that Lunenburg is the one place to build and outfit a ship.*

— *CHRONICLE HERALD*, AUGUST 23, 1960

If ever a community was ready, willing and able to take on a shipbuilding challenge, it was Lunenburg, Nova Scotia. Lunenburg's protected harbour sits snugly chiselled into Nova Scotia's rocky South Shore, just over an hour's drive from the provincial capital Halifax. Lunenburgers have a long, intimate and storied relationship with the sea.

The town of Lunenburg, Nova Scotia.

Originally, Lunenburg was a Mi'kmaq encampment called Mirliguèche that grew when the Catholic Acadian (French) settlers formed alliances with the native peoples in the mid-1700s. At the time, Britain and France were vying for supremacy in this part of the New World. Armed skirmishes were frequent, and history records a bloody and often lethal struggle for control of the area. Seeking to anchor their presence on this shore, the British organized Protestant settlers to come from Switzerland and Germany in 1753. They were mostly farmers, but within a generation the settlers adapted to harvesting the ocean. They cut local timber and became expert at crafting vessels perfectly suited to their commercial needs. Lunenburg became adept at turning out sturdy fishing schooners. The most famous of them still adorns the back of the Canadian dime: *Bluenose,* the Queen of the North Atlantic fishing fleet, launched in 1921.

Work begins on Bounty's *masts, Lunenburg 1960.*

By the time Metro-Goldwyn-Mayer came calling in 1960, boatbuilding was in Lunenburg's genes. While ship construction had changed substantially in the twentieth century, there were still tradesmen in the town supremely skilled in the crafting of wooden boats. The same shipyard that had launched *Bluenose* — Smith and Rhuland — was a busy enterprise. When news of their successful *Bounty* bid arrived, Smith and Rhuland were in the process of completing seven vessels and were about to start on two sixty-foot longliners. But building *Bounty* — a four-hundred-ton, full-rigged ship — well, this was an altogether different challenge requiring a combination of skills the yard hadn't seen in a generation. The scale of the job was daunting. It was a half-million-dollar undertaking that would fuel the local economy for months to come and, if done well, would enhance Lunenburg's reputation literally all over the world.

The contract called for Smith and Rhuland to deliver a fully rigged, ocean-going replica of *Bounty* in just six months. She would be based on the plans for the original *Bounty*, blueprints that had been preserved by the British Admiralty for almost two hundred years. To outward appearances, the new *Bounty* would be a dead ringer for the original, but the twentieth-century version would be adapted for her high-profile job. She would be substantially longer and wider than the original to accommodate camera platforms and other modern necessities. Below decks would have been unrecognizable to William Bligh, with comfortable sleeping quarters, toilets, a fully equipped galley and two powerful diesel engines.

Planners began drawing up materials lists: 400,000 board feet of wood, 12 tons of screw bolts, 2.5 tons of iron spikes, 1.5 tons of oakum for caulking, 10 miles of ropes, five on-board generators, 10,000 square feet of sail canvas, 14 tons of bar iron for long bolts, 1.5 miles of wire rigging, eight pumps, six giant deep freezes for food storage, fuel and water tanks. On and on, the lists were drawn

MGM's Jim Havens on board Bounty, *1960.*

up. Last but not least: just down the coast in Shelburne, Kenneth MacAlpine and Son got the subcontract to build an exact replica of the twenty-three-foot launch used by Bligh for his miraculous open-sea voyage to East Timor following the mutiny.

MGM installed their own person on site in Lunenburg to oversee every aspect of the construction. Former US Marine Captain Jim Havens was a battle-hardened Hollywood producer and director with extensive experience in shooting sequences at sea.

He had a reputation of being a no-nonsense, "tough but fair" movie executive. Havens's job was to familiarize himself with every plank that went into *Bounty*, and when construction was complete, to sail her to the location in Tahiti and assist with the shoot.

Smith and Rhuland hired 120 men for the *Bounty* job, including every qualified carpenter they could find, eighty of them in all. Lunenburg and surrounding counties had lifetimes of shipbuilding experience on hand. A top-notch workforce was assembled. However, Lunenburg County was then walloped by two serious winter storms. This made harvesting local timber virtually impossible. Urgent purchase orders were sent out to distant lumber yards. The result: a worrying delay in getting the job started.

Laying Bounty*'s keel at the Smith and Rhuland shipyard, 1960.*

Bounty's keel was laid on March 3, 1960. A launch date of August 27 was set. The clock was ticking, and no further delays would be acceptable. Two shifts went at it, day and night. Most of the workers had never even seen a square-rigged ship in their lives, let alone worked on one. Old-timers were called in: seventy-three-year-old Gordon Wentzell and seventy-one-year-old Howard Falkenham put their retirements on hold and donned their overalls. So as to avoid further weather-related problems, *Bounty* was built inside the yard's main shed. The ship would eventually fill the building to the rafters.

Bounty's mainmast arrived in Lunenburg as a roughly squared sixty-five-foot-long piece of Douglas fir. The carpenters used traditional hand tools — the broad axe and the adze — to turn the timber into an eight-sided pole. Then, to sixteen sides, and from there they shaped and rounded the wood into what everyone could recognize as a ship's mast. No machines existed to do the job.

Outside the yard, a small army of suppliers stepped up. Dauphinee & Sons landed a huge order for hundreds of blocks

Lunenburg sailmaker Charles Hebb.

Oiled ropes destined to become Bounty's *rigging.*

and deadeyes, used to rig the ship. Lunenburg Foundry and Engineering were subcontracted to manufacture rigging and install the diesel engines.

Charles Hebb's sail loft got the job of cutting and stitching *Bounty*'s enormous canvas requirements. Hebb was the last remaining sailmaker in an operation that once employed twenty men. Hebb and his assistant Bud Lohnes used the sailmaker's leather palm and curved needle to finish the sail grommets and edging on the biggest order of their long careers.

Halifax Heating and Air Conditioning set about making sure *Bounty*'s air would be comfortable in the tropics. T. Walters and Sons, marine blacksmiths, began the huge

Launch day in Lunenburg, August 27, 1960.

job of crafting *Bounty*'s iron fittings, using traditional open-fire forging. American oak and Douglas fir from Oregon and British Columbia was imported to augment local spruce and birch. Lunenburg's streets buzzed with excitement as *Bounty* took shape. So many visitors flocked into town to get a look that Fred Rhuland had to hire a tour guide to manage the crowds, a first in the shipyard's history.

CBC Halifax filmed *Bounty*'s construction, and interviewed the builders and craftsmen involved. The resulting program, *Building HMS* Bounty, has been brilliantly preserved, and makes compelling viewing even today. The cameras capture white-hot iron being hammered in Vernon Walters's forge and a candid interview with Charles Hebb at work. The film is a superb record of the many traditional skills that went into creating *Bounty*.

CBC cameras were on hand for launch day, too. In the bright August sunshine, a crowd estimated to be ten-thousand strong lined the waterfront, and adjacent shorelines. MacKenzie Bus Lines laid on extra vehicles to handle the crowds.

People came to witness what was widely — and correctly — anticipated to be a historic occasion. The companies and subcontractors involved in the project proudly took out congratulatory ads in the newspapers. Passes for the seats on the officials' platform were the hottest tickets Lunenburg had seen in a lifetime. Premier Robert Stanfield, Mayor R. G. Wood and a bevy of guests and dignitaries were on hand.

At the podium, a tight knot of key participants gathered behind a cluster of radio microphones that carried the event live across Nova Scotia and beyond. In a clear voice, the Canadian Navy's top brass in Atlantic Canada, Rear Admiral H. F. Pullen, set a celebratory tone:

> *Today we go back 200 years to see an eighteenth-century ship launched and, in due course, rigged and ready for sea. All this is made possible by the skills and craftsman of many Lunenburgers. Truly, a wonderful achievement. May she have fair winds for all her voyages.*

Next, standing close to *Bounty*'s freshly painted, royal-blue hull, with shipyard proprietor Fred Rhuland beside him, Archdeacon Ralph Fowlow read the blessing. "Go forth, o blessed ship, and may harmony, peace and goodwill prevail in thee, and the blessing of God go with thee, through Jesus Christ our Lord, Amen."

Inside and outside the shed, heads were bowed in quiet reverence.

Then, Mrs. Margaret Rhuland — Fred's wife — stepped up. MGM's point man Jim Havens stood beside her and handed her a cloth-covered bottle. Inside the bottle: not the traditional champagne, but instead sea water from Tahiti, shipped to Lunenburg by MGM for this specific moment.

Mrs. Rhuland took a firm grip on the neck of the bottle and steadied herself. "May God be merciful to this ship. May she have supremacy over the sea and fair sailing. I christen this ship — *Bounty*."

With that Mrs. Rhuland swung her arm and smashed the bottle against the bow, giving *Bounty* her very first taste of the Pacific Ocean.

Slowly, as the work crew pounded wedges underneath *Bounty*'s hull, she started to slide backwards down the slipways. Inside the shed, the crowd shouted out three cheers. By the time *Bounty*'s stern hit the water, she was moving at a good clip. Every horn in Lunenburg harbour sounded off in salute, and the crowd roared their approval.

As CBC announcer Gerry Fogarty put it in *Building the* Bounty: "The job of building her was only half completed. As yet she was just a hull. Faithful to be sure, but lacking the mast, the yards and the sails that would give her purpose and beauty."

Rigging *Bounty* as she was tied to the dock in Lunenburg took a month. According to tradition and sailor superstition, a silver dollar was placed under the base of the mainmast as it was lowered into position.

After that, sea trials began, and to everyone's satisfaction and relief, *Bounty* performed well under sail. But delays were starting to mount up.

MGM's tough-guy Jim Havens loosened up enough to give an interview to CBC Television: "The craftsman here in Lunenburg are the best I've ever seen in the shipbuilding profession. They can take a raw piece of timber, put the broad axe and adze to work, and fashion out a stern post, a rudder, a frame or anything else in a short time. I think these people are to be complemented on the job they've done."

Captain Ellsworth Coggins from Dartmouth was chosen as *Bounty*'s captain. The crew selected to take *Bounty* to Tahiti — some of whom helped to build her — was composed almost

Bounty*'s hull afloat on launch day, ready for masts and rigging.*

completely of Nova Scotian men, from seafaring towns all
over the province including Bridgewater, Parrsboro, Liverpool,
Hantsport, Oyster Pond, Halifax and Dartmouth. Last-minute
difficulties in finding a First Mate delayed departure for a few
days, until Ross MacKay was hired and driven at full speed from
Amherst to Lunenburg.

On October 26, 1960, watched by journalists and photographers
from all over the country, *Bounty* cast off. Three of the crew pumped
out a spirited rendition of the popular song "Now Is the Hour,"
accompanied by violin, guitar and accordion. Motoring slowly past
the squat, red-and-white lighthouse on Battery Point, *Bounty* had at
last begun her seven-thousand-mile journey to Tahiti.

Lewis Jannex from Oyster Pond stood at the ship's wheel —
the exact wheel that Errol Flynn had stood beside in the 1935

film. MGM had kept the wheel in a safe place and had arranged for it to be installed on this brand new Lunenburg *Bounty*.

MGM took out a full-page ad in the *Halifax Chronicle Herald*. "We appreciate the tremendous interest that has been shown by all of Canada in the building of the *Bounty* . . . Those concerned with the production are determined that *Mutiny on the Bounty* will be one of the greatest motion pictures ever made."

Meanwhile, on the other side of the world in the Pacific, the film crew had already been assembled. Shooting with *Bounty* was supposed to have started already, to take advantage of the late September and October weather. Marlon Brando was warring with the producers and director over the script — the early signs of what would become a nightmare for the film studio in its dealings with their lead actor. Writers were hired, then fired. Nervous MGM accountants started to add up the costs of the delays. The film started out with an enormous budget (for the time) of $10 million. It wouldn't be enough. Not nearly enough.

CHAPTER 7
The *Bounty* Boys

"I signed on the Bounty *mainly to get the adventure. It seems like a wonderful opportunity to get in the South Seas, which must be everyone's dream at one time or another. I can hardly wait to get there. They say those golden-skinned girls down there are really pretty."*

— HUGH BOYD, *BOUNTY* CREW MEMBER
(INTERVIEWED BY CBC TV, SEPTEMBER 1960)

Lunenburg's *Bounty* almost didn't make it to Tahiti.

Bounty *crew member Hugh Boyd.*

Two weeks out of Nova Scotia, she reached the Panama Canal. During a brief stopover in Panama, *Bounty* picked up an extra passenger who had pleaded with MGM to be allowed on board. He was a renowned travel writer from *National Geographic* magazine, Luis Marden.

Just a few years prior, Marden had dived onto HMAV *Bounty*'s wreck in Pitcairn. Among the artifacts he recovered were some eighteenth-century bronze sheathing nails. In Panama, Marden had one of those nails with him. He hammered the nail into the hull of Lunenburg's *Bounty* so that, in his words, "the old ship contributed at least a small portion to her namesake."

The Panama Canal route spared Captain Coggin's *Bounty* the ordeal of going around Cape Horn as William Bligh had attempted to do 175 years earlier. But no one could have anticipated the calamity that happened next. Crossing the equator, *Bounty*'s brand-new pumps were switched on to move diesel fuel from a reserve tank into the main tank. Under pressure, a rubber hose burst, spewing diesel over a hot engine block. Luis Marden recorded in his November 21, 1960, journal entry what happened next:

> *An alarm went off and we heard the cry 'Fire in the engine room!' We dashed into the passage, which was rapidly filling with smoke. I was ordered on deck where I found most of crew in lifejackets mustering forward and taking covers off boats. Smoke pouring out of the aft ventilators.*

Fire down below is a nightmare for any vessel at sea. Captain Coggins sent out SOS messages. Three nearby commercial ships responded. Crewman John Kendall from Windsor, NS, later told the *Halifax Herald* that as crew members fought the fire, the flames burned through wiring, shutting down the pump and the flow of leaking fuel. That was a lucky break. Within twenty

Captain Ellsworth Coggins at Bounty's *navigation table, en route to Tahiti in 1960.*

minutes, the fire was brought under control. On deck, the mate and engineer were retching from smoke inhalation. MGM's Jim Havens received bad burns to his left forearm. But miraculously, *Bounty* had averted a fiery end. It wouldn't be the last time this would happen.

The only other problem encountered on the voyage was chronic seasickness. Because of the way she had been rigged for film work, *Bounty* was top-heavy and rolled frighteningly in heavy seas. The motion took its toll on most of the men on board, even the most seasoned among them.

On location, ready for the cameras to roll. At centre, Marlon Brando.

When *Bounty* arrived in Tahiti on December 3, 1960, the crew was greeted in the manner they had hoped for. Large war canoes paddled out from shore. Hundreds of locals came out to welcome *Bounty*'s crew with music, kisses and flower leis. MGM publicists had done their jobs.

Once settled in, the business of shooting film began. For the crew this meant early rising, with twelve-hour days on the water, six days a week. They did double duty, not only operating the ship but also appearing as background performers. No one had had a haircut since Lunenburg. The film's stylists required them to sport eighteen-century-style pigtails on the back of their heads. John Kendall — who played the part of ship's cooper — wrote to his wife complaining that the days were monotonous. An entire day could be spent rehearsing one shot over and over again, he wrote, "just for a shot that will last a minute on the screen." More like fifteen seconds. That's the hurry-up-and-wait reality of movie making.

If things were difficult for the Lunenburg boys, they were much worse for MGM. Marlon Brando was scaling new heights of obstinacy. He appeared to be going out of his way to sabotage the movie. The magazine *The Saturday Evening Post* would later publish a piece entitled "The Mutiny of Marlon Brando." It describes in excruciating detail the plight of MGM, which was paying the price for giving "a ham actor, a petulant child, complete control of an expensive picture." British co-star Trevor Howard told a reporter: "[Brando] was unprofessional and absolutely ridiculous."

At one point, after shooting had commenced, Brando told MGM he had decided he no longer wanted to play the part of Fletcher Christian at all. He was more interested in playing Pitcairn survivor Alexander Smith. The film's distinguished English director — Sir Carol Reed — quit the film. More delays. The replacement director, Lewis Milestone, told *The Saturday Evening Post:* "I've never seen anything like it. Did you ever hear of an actor who put plugs in his ears so he couldn't listen to the director or the other actors? That's what Brando did."

Marlon Brando was getting paid $25,000 a week. He lived in a luxurious villa, stayed up late carousing, and frequently showed up for work bleary-eyed, unprepared and argumentative. Brando debated every shot before the cameras rolled. In stark contrast, the Lunenburg crew had no say in anything, and made $500 a week. Some of them were getting fed up. Others were homesick.

Because of enormous public interest in Nova Scotia, CBC Halifax sent a film crew to Tahiti to document the event. *Bounty's* Nova Scotian crew were filmed at work, and also on their days

Left: Bounty's *messboy Wayne Dewar serves up a plate of food.*
Right: *Dewar in full wardrobe as a British naval officer.*

off, shopping for souvenirs, and attending a traditional Tahitian barbeque hosted by locals. As it had been for Bligh's sailors on the original HMAV *Bounty*, romance was in the Tahitian air.

One of *Bounty*'s crew was nineteen-year-old Wayne Dewar, from Hantsport, Nova Scotia.

Dewar signed on as mess boy, helping to feed the crew but hungry himself for a South Seas adventure. The morning he left his home in Nova Scotia, his mother thought she saw an omen: a black crow flying across her verandah. She begged Wayne not to go, but there was no stopping him.

Wayne's arrival in Tahiti met all his expectations. He was photographed flanked by two young Tahitian women, a picture he sent back to his father and that made its way onto the pages of the Halifax newspaper. Once in Tahiti, like most of *Bounty's* crew, Wayne was employed as an extra, or background performer. Working on a film set was like nothing he had ever experienced, and the much-vaunted hospitality of Tahitians quickly became an intoxicating reality.

Dewar was outgoing and charming, and cut a handsome figure in his eighteenth-century costume. Before long, he was selected by the filmmakers as Marlon Brando's official stand-in.

On a beach one moonlit night, Wayne struck up a conversation with one of the Polynesian female performers working on set. A contemporary newspaper account of the meeting describes the woman as having "a smile that sparkles like pearls, a temper like a tropical storm, and a charm as enchanting as the island of Tahiti." Her name was Teretiaiti Teyahineheipoua Maifano, a twenty-four-year-old nurse, daughter of a pearl diver, recruited by MGM to play the part of a Tahitian dancer. Wayne Dewar was smitten. They fell in love, and their whirlwind romance changed both their lives forever. Teretiaiti had no way of knowing it on that moonlit beach, but she would soon leave Tahiti to spend the rest of her life in Nova Scotia.

Marlon Brando himself was interviewed by CBC Halifax announcer Jack MacAndrew, in what must have seemed like a journalistic coup at the time. As it turned out, Brando provided a rambling, offhand and unfocused interview. Star power being what it is, CBC felt obliged to include it in their film.

But among all the examples of his difficult behaviour on the movie set, Brando was to take one particularly defiant stand that more than any other shaped the rest of the *Bounty* story.

In the final climactic scene of their epic film, MGM's production plan called for the Lunenburg-built *Bounty* to be set ablaze, burned and sunk, just as Fletcher Christian and his group had done to the original in 1790. By now, Brando had somehow managed to split his affections between his female Tahitian co-

CBC Halifax announcer Jack MacAndrew interviews Marlon Brando on set.

star and the ship herself. He issued an ultimatum: if MGM burned *Bounty,* he would not finish the film. MGM had no real choice but to acquiesce. So, they created a smaller model *Bounty,* to be set alight for the scene.

Lunenburg's *Bounty* escaped certain destruction and would sail another fifty years. Her beautiful lines would be admired all over the world, thanks to the enigmatic actor who went on to star in *The Ugly American.*

CHAPTER 8
A Movie Star

If Metro-Goldwyn-Mayer were going to be stuck with *Bounty*, they figured she might as well be put to work. Studio publicists organized a "world tour" designed to give the film a boost at the box office. In the next seven months, *Bounty* would sail some thirty thousand nautical miles, halfway around the world and back again.

In the fall of 1961, she sailed across the Pacific to Long Beach, California, where she was given a starlet's welcome. Industry gossip about trouble on the movie's set only piqued additional curiosity. After wintering in Long Beach, and a minor refit, *Bounty* began her world tour. Heading north, *Bounty* battled fifty-knot winds to

Bounty *at sea.*

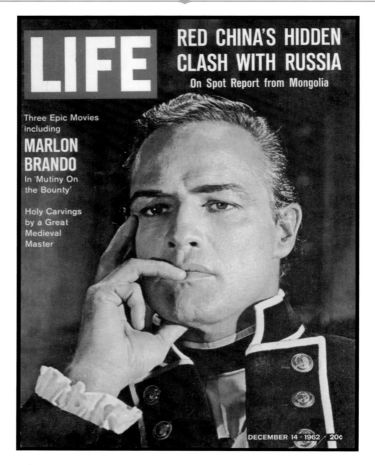

Life *magazine cover, 1962.*

visit Vancouver, BC. The *Vancouver Sun* reported on June 16, 1962, that an astonishing 350,000 people turned out to greet her. British Columbians in four hundred small craft swarmed around her as *Bounty* motored under the Lion's Gate Bridge. Clearly, the ship had mass appeal.

On July 4 — US Independence Day — she sailed into San Francisco Bay. Huge crowds thronged the waterfront to see her. It was becoming apparent that a fully equipped square-rigged ship was a curiosity that few could resist.

In the late summer, *Bounty*'s adventures continued in the Caribbean, where the crew found themselves menaced by six giant

Bounty *visits Vancouver, 1962.*

waterspouts. Just before one of them struck *Bounty*'s stern, it veered off. A close call. From there, she headed across the Atlantic to France. En route, *Bounty* was hit by a fierce squall that split three of her sails. In the English Channel, she narrowly avoided a collision

A display case showing Bounty *costumes worn by Charles Laughton, Clark Gable, Trevor Howard and Marlon Brando in MGM's films.*

when a merchant ship cut across her bow. *Bounty* was continuing her run of near misses and good luck.

In September 1962, *Bounty* made her first visit to the motherland of her ancestor. In Dover harbour, she was greeted with a twenty-one-gun salute. Britons were hugely attracted by this curiosity of UK naval history. After that, *Bounty* made an appearance on the Thames, towed by tugboat to the Pool of London. With symbolic Royal Assent, she anchored near Tower Bridge.

If it wasn't obvious to MGM before — it was now. Lunenburg's *Bounty* was a huge draw wherever she went. Studio heads had to wonder: could Marlon Brando have been right all along? Would it have been a crime to have burned such a strong link to a vanished era? Whatever emotion *Bounty* was tapping into — some sort of rich vein of nostalgia and romanticism — it had to be good for business.

Bounty said goodbye to her British admirers and headed back to New York for the movie's premiere. MGM was nervous. Would their bloated epic *Mutiny on the Bounty* give a lift to the studio's fortunes? Or would it sink them?

CHAPTER 9
Bounty Hits the Big Screen

As surely as Lunenburg's *Bounty* slid down the slipways at the Smith and Rhuland shipyard, MGM's epic new film experienced a similar downward trajectory at the box office. The film had come in at $19 million, almost twice the studio's original budget. The only hope now was for blockbuster business at the theatres. The film opened in November 1962 to decidedly mixed reviews. Some critics liked the grand sweep of the spectacle. Others found the film bloated. Brando's oddball portrayal of Fletcher Christian as a foppish English aristocrat came in for some harsh criticism.

> *There is so much in this picture that is stirring and beautiful that it is painful to note and call attention to the fact that it also has faults. But it has, and the most obvious of them is the way Marlon Brando makes Fletcher Christian an eccentric who dominates the entire dramatic scheme . . . The effect is extremely disconcerting . . . through the first two hours of this uncomfortably three-hour-long picture . . .*
> — New York Times, *November 9, 1962*

Nonetheless, the film was admired for its exotic setting, stunning cinematography and terrific story.

One place where audience expectations were running high was Nova Scotia. After openings in New York, Los Angeles, Toronto and Montreal, Halifax's turn came months later on the evening of March 29, 1963. It was quite the occasion, the

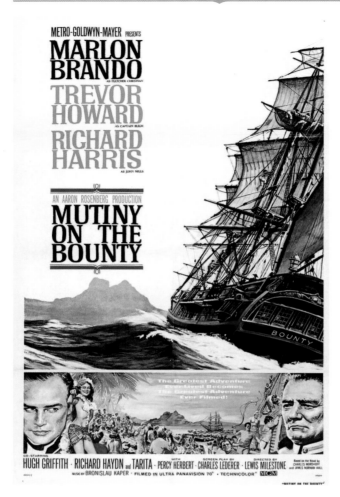

Mutiny on the
Bounty *movie
poster, 1962.*

excitement having been fuelled by a contest on CHNS Radio that
rewarded listeners for correctly answering the question: "Where
was *Bounty* built?"

CBC Television covered the premiere, sending talk-show host
Libby Christensen and a camera crew to the Paramount Theatre on
Barrington Street. *Bounty's* Captain Ellsworth Coggins, shipbuilder
Fred Rhuland, CBC's Jack MacAndrew, and several of *Bounty's*
Tahiti crew were among the guests of honour interviewed under
the bright camera lights. In this audience, there was a palpable
sense of pride in the work done by Lunenburg's shipwrights three
years prior.

Mutiny on the Bounty *posters from the Italian and French releases, 1962.*

"For pure fictional entertainment I thought it was terrific," premiere attendee Jack Brailey told CBC. "I thought some of the scenes in it were wonderful and I felt thrilled at the first scene of the *Bounty* sailing, when the whole Nova Scotia audience applauded simultaneously. It was the most spontaneous demonstration I've ever seen in a movie [theatre]."

There was another special guest in attendance that night, a small Tahitian woman, warmly dressed in a white fur coat: Teretiaiti Maifano. Now known to everyone as Suzanne, she stood in the CBC camera lights beside the mess boy she had fallen for on that moonlit night back home.

Suzanne and Wayne Dewar had travelled together from Tahiti to Los Angeles, to work on the movie's final scenes. During the shoot, they eloped and were married in Las Vegas.

Libby Christensen: "How do you find life in our part of the world Suzanne? Did you find the winter cold?"
Suzanne Dewar (giggling): "Oh yes, I was almost frozen."
Christensen: "Do you think you can stand it though? Do you think you're going to enjoy living in Nova Scotia?"
Dewar: "Oh I think so, yes, I like it here."
Christensen: "You must be pleased to hear that, Wayne?"
Wayne Dewar: "Oh yes!"
(They all laugh together)

Tahitian Suzanne Dewar at Bounty's *premiere in Halifax.*

That evening, the Dewars and others would have spotted Wayne in the background of the shot as the climactic *Bounty* mutiny scene played out on the Technicolor screen. Suzanne Dewar was the first Tahitian immigrant to Nova Scotia to become a Canadian citizen.

The other 1963 Nova Scotia screening that caused a local sensation was the one at the Capitol Theatre on Lincoln Street in Lunenburg. The theatre manager, Arthur Corkum, received explicit instructions regarding the film's presentation and marketing from MGM's offices in Toronto and New York.

"Have ordered a print which we expect shortly. As this is a new print, please have your operator use extreme care in handling," wrote MGM's Eric Golding. "As you no doubt know, Halifax is doing exceptional business, and you may expect similar reaction."

Suzanne Dewar, pictured at home in 1999.

In 1963, Suzanne Dewar was initially treated as something of a celebrity in Hantsport, Nova Scotia. "Everybody wanted to look at me to see if I was real . . ." she told the *Halifax Herald* in 1999. She also shared that despite being welcomed by the community, she had not found true happiness in her new home. Wayne worked for a local gypsum company and was frequently away on ships. Their marriage lasted until 1966. Suzanne worked at the Polynesian Room restaurant in Halifax and the Holiday Inn, and later became a caregiver. She said her biggest regret was losing touch with her family in Tahiti, and that she was never able to go back there for a visit. Suzanne died in Halifax in 2010. The two children she had with Wayne now live in Florida.

From MGM's Toronto office to Arthur Corkum, dated April 10, 1963:

> *All of your advertising should carry copy: LIMITED ENGAGEMENT. We feel it is not good to announce in advance it is a two-week engagement because many people will continue to put off attending until it is too late. It is better to let them think it will play only a few days or a week to make sure your theatre is filled.*

April 10, 1963

Mr. Arthur Corkum,
Capitol Theatre,
Lunenburg, N.S.

Dear Mr. Corkum:

Attached is the suggested advertising budget for your engagement of MUTINY ON
THE BOUNTY. I have set it up to the best of my ability with the knowledge I
have of your situation, and knowing that just about everyone in your area will
want to see this picture.

If either you or Mr. Spencer feel anything should be altered in this advertising
schedule please let me know immediately.

I have sent the following material to you:

Ad mats – 2 mats of #211.
         1 mat of #214 – proofs of these ads are enclosed.
         1 mat of #381

Scene mats – 1 mat of each: 2-A; 2-D; 4-A; 4-B; 3-C; 3-B; and 3 mats of 2-F.
         Trust you will be able to get these scene mats planted in your papers
         free of charge.

1 spot announcement recording for your radio (this will be forwarded by Jim
                 McDonough in Halifax)

1 40x60 (this is sent gratis. Perhaps you can mount it and use it at front of theatre.

15 Souvenir books.   These are sent to you gratis and are to be given to those
         people in newspapers, radio stations, etc. who will help with your promotion.

10 1-sheets (5 of these have the cast and 5 do not).

1 set   Rome Lithos.   These are beautiful things and I know you will make good
         use of them around the theatre or in windows in your town.

*MGM's correspondence with Lunenburg's Capitol Theatre manager
Arthur Corkum.*

Ads were taken out in all the regional weekly papers. Posters, post cards and special MGM souvenir booklets were dispatched to Lunenburg. Business at the Capitol was brisk for the entire two-week run. Whatever people elsewhere said or thought about the film, in the minds of Nova Scotians the real star of the film was *Bounty* herself, and she had performed magnificently. So successful was the

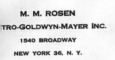

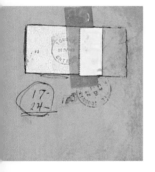

ship, that even as the popcorn machines popped for *Bounty* fans at the Capitol Theatre, Smith and Rhuland's yard on the Lunenburg waterfront was already crafting another incarnation of a famous vessel from a bygone era: the schooner *Bluenose II*.

Mutiny on the Bounty was nominated for five Academy Awards, but won none. In the end, MGM took a multimillion-dollar loss on the film.

One thing remained: the 412-ton *Bounty* herself. What was to become of her? MGM — having been thwarted in their plan to burn *Bounty* during filming — was now stuck with her.

Bounty was unwanted and — for the time being at least — homeless.

CHAPTER 10
A Show Boat

Come on board the Bounty. *Relive above and below decks the thoughts of the men who struggled to escape tyranny and cruelty for the solitude peace and serenity of Tahiti — Pearl of the seven seas. And be sure to bring your camera! You will always want to remember the* Bounty, *the most beautiful sailing ship afloat.*

— MGM'S TOURIST BROCHURE, ST. PETERSBURG, FLORIDA

The HMS Bounty restaurant in Los Angeles.

To their credit, Metro-Goldwyn-Mayer tried to do right by *Bounty*.

Bounty's film-related duties were over, and now the studio just wanted to quietly part with their increasingly famous but needy movie property. *Bounty* was tied to the dock at San Pedro, the port area of Los Angeles. San Pedro has a rich maritime history going back to 1542. The area changed hands from Spain, to Mexico and eventually to the United States. It grew into an important naval base and, in 1963, developers were working on a tourist-oriented idea called Ports O'Call. *Bounty* found herself tied up beside a waterfront restaurant, the newest attraction in a storied harbour. To this day, Los Angeles still maintains her *Bounty* connection through a neighbourhood restaurant on Wilshire Boulevard, a purveyor of "Food and Grog."

In 1963, MGM was open to the idea of simply giving *Bounty* away to a good home. The now-famous square-rigger was valued at $650,000. MGM entertained pitches from an oddball assortment of commercial ventures and hucksters. A nightclub in Polynesia wanted her. The Wilson Steamship Company of Washington, DC, wanted to use *Bounty* to stimulate youth interest in US history and inland waterways. The Shaw Steamship Co. of Halifax, NS, offered to trade another ship and $100,000 cash to take possession of *Bounty*. A concert promoter from Burbank California had plans to use *Bounty* to raise money for charitable causes. MGM looked at the options and ended up offering *Bounty* to the government of Canada — at no charge. The conditions were that Canada would take full ownership and financial responsibility, sail *Bounty* through the Panama Canal and take her up the eastern seaboard, probably back to Nova Scotia. There, the Canadian Navy would have to take over *Bounty*'s operation and operate her as a sail-training ship for a minimum of one year.

The Canadian Navy passed on the opportunity. For all of *Bounty*'s photogenic qualities, there were questions about the

New York World's Fair, 1964.

practicality of maintaining and insuring her. Ultimately, MGM decided to hang on to *Bounty* until a proper solution could be found.

In 1964, *Bounty* took part in the New York World's Fair. The pilot who brought her into the harbour was legendary New York ship pilot James Stillwagon. Stillwagon was given all the tricky, high-profile harbour assignments of the day. MGM wanted publicity photos of their ship sailing into New York, but the wind wasn't cooperating. The sails were hanging flat. In a moment of inspiration, Stillwagon put *Bounty*'s two powerful motors into reverse. Heading backwards, the sails billowed beautifully for the cameras. In later years, Stillwagon's son would remember that, while his dad filled the sails, *Bounty*'s wake was coming off the bow — not the stern.

At the World's Fair, nestled behind a faux-tropical paradise pavilion, *Bounty* had her share of the eventual fifty-one million visitors. She was a bit of a misfit in an international exhibition that showcased mid-twentieth-century technological advances. The World's Fair was much more about the Space Age than the Age of Sail.

Still, Robert Moses, President of the World's Fair, enthused about *Bounty:* "It is the real thing. It is the authentic thing. People miss this sort of adventure saga in the age of aircraft. This is romance."

The *Washington Daily News* wrote: "Your children's children will not see her like again. Nor will you."

Not the ship, perhaps. But definitely related souvenirs. *Bounty* paperweights from 1964 are now collectors' items and are still bought and sold on eBay.

Bounty poster from New York World's Fair, 1964.

After her run at the New York World's Fair, MGM finally decided on a long-term strategy for *Bounty*. She was sent south to Florida, to her new (and permanent) home in St. Petersburg.

Bounty was tied to the dock in Vinoy Basin, not far from the city's municipal pier. She was to become the centrepiece of an MGM South Sea exhibit, complete with a breadfruit plant imported especially for the purpose. The idea was to give paying visitors a glimpse into the past. MGM made the display as immersive as they could and rang the cash registers as the tourists came aboard.

The rigging was freshly tarred. Down below, *Bounty* was furnished with faux eighteenth-century fittings and furnishings, including weather-worn sea-chests, pewter tableware, wooden barrels and canvas hammocks. The designers' intent was to show *Bounty* "as if Bligh's crew had just left the ship for shore leave." Inevitably, creative liberties were taken and historical accuracy was not high on the list of priorities.

The captain's "grand cabin" — denied to William Bligh in 1787 so that breadfruit seedlings could be accommodated — was furnished with antiques from other ships and presented as Bligh's personal quarters. Full-size wax figures in naval uniforms were installed to represent Christian and Bligh.

Bounty tied to the dock in St. Petersburg, Florida.

The finishing touch was an audio playback of voices that repeated on a loop: a conversation between Bligh and Christian, taken from the soundtrack of the 1935 MGM film.

Bounty settled into her life as a marine-historical attraction, open daily from 9 a.m. until 10 p.m. The adjoining gift shop did brisk business, selling "rare Pitcairn Island woodcarvings, handmade by direct descendants of the mutineers." Scrimshaw carvings on whale teeth, reproductions of the ship's furnishings and postage stamps from Pitcairn Islands were also on display.

Occasionally, MGM's entertainment division found ways to get *Bounty* out on the water. In 1965, *Bounty* appeared on TV alongside the world's most famous dolphin, in a new MGM television series, *Flipper.* The episode, entitled "Flipper and the *Bounty*," provides an interesting record of what *Bounty* looked like in her prime, above and below decks.

In 1983, *Bounty* was again pressed into service for the UK/US comedy *Yellowbeard,* which starred a dazzling array of British and American comedic talent, including some of the Monty Python troupe, Cheech and Chong and the much-loved-but-very-odd Marty Feldman, who actually died during the making of the movie. No one cared about historical verisimilitude — this was a chaotic, madcap comedy.

Parkin Christian – a direct descendant of Fletcher Christian – inspects Bounty *at the 1964 New York World's Fair.*

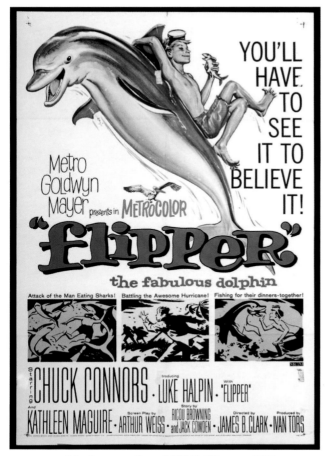

Movie poster from MGM's Flipper, *1963.*

So *Bounty* played the part of both a Spanish galleon and a Royal Naval frigate. With just a hint of pride, John Cleese would later observe that "*Yellowbeard* is one of the six worst movies made in the history of the world."

Through the 1970s and 80s, international travellers, Boy Scouts, convention delegates and tourists from every continent clambered on board *Bounty* while she was tied up at her home in St. Petersburg. Many people had their picture taken beside her giant ship's wheel. If the ship wasn't actually going very far, she at least sparked the imaginations of literally hundreds of thousands of visitors.

In 1986, a different spark of the imagination changed *Bounty*'s fortunes. American broadcasting mogul Ted Turner was in acquisition mode. Turner had amassed a fortune through his Turner Broadcasting System, and his CNN television channel had proved to be a profitable game changer in the TV news business. He purchased two sports franchises — the Atlanta Braves and the Atlanta Hawks. Always looking to expand, Turner tried but failed to buy CBS. Then he trained his sights on MGM/United Artists. It made perfect sense, dovetailing with his

Ted Turner — yachting enthusiast, cable news tycoon and Bounty's *new owner.*

notion of founding a cable channel dedicated to classic movies. In a monster deal valued at $1.5 billion, Turner became the new owner of MGM's corporate assets, including a movie lot in Culver City, and MGM's film and television library.

But buried inside the deal was a small-print surprise for Turner. He started to receive invoices for the maintenance, upkeep and docking of a three-masted ship in Florida. To his bemusement, along with the catalogue of MGM's films, Turner had unwittingly acquired *Bounty* herself. To shed some debt, Turner divested himself of MGM/UA and the studio lot. But he kept the MGM film library, and the now twenty-six-year-old, floating movie star.

Turner was a yachting enthusiast. In 1977, he had competed against other syndicates of millionaires and corporations, and successfully defended the America's Cup. Money was no object for the businessman, and *Bounty* was something of a conversation piece

Bounty *at anchor.*

for him. He put some money into fixing her up and sent her off on a new series of adventures. *Bounty*'s first stop was New York City, part of the parade of ships attending the official state celebration of the Statue of Liberty Centennial. Also attending that July 4 in 1986 was *Bounty*'s Smith and Rhuland Lunenburg soulmate, the schooner *Bluenose II.*

A few years later, Turner was instrumental in getting *Bounty* off the dock in St. Petersburg again and back onto the big screen.

In 1990, his own production company produced a new version of *Treasure Island*, starring Charlton Heston. The film was panned by the critics, but the vertical integration was perfect: Ted Turner used his own wooden tall ship to star in his own adventure movie, to play on his own television channel.

By now, *Bounty* had become a participant in gatherings of tall ships. These events were just taking hold in the mid-1980s, drawing participants from around the world. *Bounty* was much smaller and less well provided for than many of the bigger ships, but her piratical aspect always drew a crowd at tall-ship waterfront festivals, which today are both big business and massively attended events.

Inevitably, for Ted Turner the novelty of owning a square-rigger eventually wore off. *Bounty* was now showing her age. Her upkeep was expensive. She needed some serious refitting, and Turner — ever the astute businessman — decided he wasn't the one to do it. Instead, he would simply give her away to a good home, and maybe get a tax deduction at the same time.

In 1993, after all the competing bids were examined, the winner was declared to be a small, seafaring town just south of Boston: Fall River, Massachusetts. The town's Chamber of Commerce was jubilant at their good fortune.

They had no idea of the trouble they were getting into.

CHAPTER 11
A Slow Decline

"A boat is a hole in the water that you pour money into."
— BOAT OWNERS' ADAGE

There's an oft-repeated saying in the sailing community that the two happiest days in boat owners' lives are the day they buy a boat, and the day they sell it. This certainly proved true for the community of Fall River, Massachusetts, and their seven-year entanglement with *Bounty*. What started out in 1993 looking like an exciting commercial opportunity ended up in a pile of bills and the bitter taste of disappointment.

Bounty *approaches her new home in Fall River, Massachusetts.*

Excitement on board as Bounty *sails up the Taunton River in Massachusetts, June 21, 1993.*

Fall River was once the epicentre of the cotton textile industry in New England, a veritable boomtown in the nineteenth century. Migrant workers poured in to keep the mills humming. In 1871 and 1872 alone, more than twenty-thousand new inhabitants moved in, predominantly Irish and French Canadians. Fall River was an economic engine that just kept on growing. Until it didn't. Competition from mills in the southern United States, falling demand for cotton in the 1920s and the Great Depression of the 1930s all hit hard, and the town of Fall River faced bankruptcy.

Down but never out, Fall River struggled on. These days, Fall River is a community of around ninety thousand people, proud of their Portuguese, Greek and French heritage. The town is also justly proud of its long maritime history. In 1968, the community opened a well-stocked museum dedicated to the history of seafaring. It sits adjacent to Battleship Cove, a huge floating display of ships, the centrepiece of which is the Second World War battleship USS *Massachusetts*, which saw action in Iwo Jima and Okinawa. To

USS Massachusetts *welcomes* Bounty *to Fall River with cannon fire.*

most people in Fall River in 1993, *Bounty* would have represented a desirable addition to the town's impressive collection of ships, a living memorial to the age of sail. They had beaten forty bids from other communities, even Ted Turner's home town of Savannah, GA, and by god, they were going to put *Bounty* — the tourist magnet — to good use.

On June 21, 1993, *Bounty* sailed up the Taunton River to a rapturous reception. Five thousand well-wishers lined the riverbanks to get a good look at the famous three-master. Guns cracked from the USS *Massachusetts*. A flotilla of pleasure craft circled *Bounty*. The state's Lieutenant Governor Paul Cellucci gushed to reporters:

"Now Massachusetts has at least one certified movie star living here." Robert Boiselle, the president of the Fall River Chamber of Commerce, beamed with pleasure as he watched the arrival of his town's prize catch. *Bounty* would be a cornerstone of the town's effort to revitalize its sagging economy. Cameras clicked, drinks flowed, music played and couples joined hands in Portuguese contra dancing. Surely, this would go down as a good day in Fall River's long history.

"Captain Bligh" entertains tourists.

Ted Turner had donated *Bounty* to the Fall River Chamber Foundation, a body related to but separate from the town's Chamber of Commerce. In turn, *Bounty* would be operated by a separate non-profit organization, the Tall Ship *Bounty* Foundation. Exempt from US federal income tax, the foundation's mission was to turn *Bounty* into a fully functioning sail-training school. *Bounty* could operate as a seagoing laboratory for oceanography studies. Dockside, she could offer courses in everything from diesel mechanics to woodworking. And, not incidentally, she could attract tourists and help fuel the local economy.

"The people of Fall River have weathered many dark economic storms," read the editorial in Fall River's *Herald News*. "Finally, we caught a break." If only it were that simple. When *Bounty* arrived in 1993, she was in need of some serious fixing up. By now she was thirty-three years old, and she was a tired wooden ship.

In order to get certification from the US Coast Guard to take on her mission as a maritime academy, *Bounty* needed an estimated

Fall River volunteer works on Bounty.

$1.5 million in upgrades. In the meantime, *Bounty* spent the first summer in Fall River tied to the dock in Battleship Cove, attracting visitors and maybe — in the eyes of the business community — even investors.

The grand designs didn't turn out as planned. The costs of maintaining and operating *Bounty* were close to a million dollars a year. Revenues came nowhere close to covering the bills. *Bounty* was patched up to the extent the available funds allowed. She left

Bounty's *skipper Captain Robin Walbridge.*

the dock with a crew on board — but no members of the paying public, and with no Coast Guard certification to operate as a school. Instead, she was licensed as a "moored attraction vessel," which meant that visitors could only come on board while *Bounty* was securely tied up ashore.

Cracks in the veneer of support for *Bounty* began to show as early as 1994. In October, with the ship facing a new $90,000 repair bill, one Fall River councillor claimed that the town had put an "obscene" amount of money into the ship and threatened "a real mutiny on the *Bounty.*" Other locals were not happy with the fact that *Bounty* would be heading south for the winter, away from home for months at a time.

In 1995, a new captain was hired. Robin Walbridge was a native of *Bounty*'s former home in St. Petersburg, FL. Walbridge was an able mechanic, someone who could fix almost anything. He was also an experienced mariner. He had been an instructor, training navy crews on "Old Ironsides," the legendary USS *Constitution.* Walbridge loved ships, and he quickly came to love *Bounty.* He took her out to harbour festivals and tall-ship events, as much as operational funding permitted. In 1997, *Bounty* toured the eastern seaboard and attracted crowds in multiple ports including Rochester, NY; Quebec City, QC; Montreal, QC; and Kingston, Ontario. People paid to come on board — $8 a head, $4 for children — but there was never enough money to properly refurbish the ship. Foremost among her problems: *Bounty* leaked. All wooden vessels are prone to leakage through the seams in their wooden hulls. Routinely, bilge pumps remedy the situation. But the truth is that *Bounty* leaked more than most and, though it was increasingly a problem, Walbridge did the best he could and sailed on.

In 1997, *Bounty* got an overhaul costing $250,000 in Fairhaven, Massachusetts. It was something, but not nearly enough. In the world of tall-ship repair, a quarter of a million dollars doesn't go all that far.

By the summer of 1998, open dissent about the merits of keeping *Bounty* had broken out in Fall River. A *Herald News* editorial published in June pulled no punches: "As we did upon its glorious arrival in Fall River, we hope today that the *Bounty* will survive. But it must do so through its own devices, without the support of tax payers. The city, the state, even the feds have coddled the *Bounty* for too long. Now it's time for it to sink or swim."

Just four months later, in October, 1998, *Bounty* very nearly did sink. She was involved in a close call, en route to St. Petersburg for the winter. Off the coast of North Carolina, water started to rise in the engine room. This was no small leak. Seawater was pouring in. Walbridge called the Coast Guard. Portable water pumps were loaded onto Coast Guard helicopters and flown out to *Bounty*. Navy ships in the vicinity stood by. More pumps arrived on a US Coast Guard cutter. For a while things were tense, but Walbridge would not abandon ship. The crew stayed on board. The multiple pumps were eventually able to move more water out than was coming in through the hull, and *Bounty* was towed to port. It was a wake-up call for

Ice accumulates on Bounty's *hull in Fall River, Massachusetts.*

everyone, including the Tall Ship *Bounty* Foundation in Fall River. The ship needed expensive repairs, but the money just wasn't there. Things were getting bad, and they were only going to get worse.

The *Herald News* columnist Marc Munroe Dion vented his personal frustration while *Bounty* was — again — away from her homeport. In a column headlined "There she was . . . gone," Dion wrote: "I have hope. Every night, while Fall River sleeps, I drive down to the waterfront and look to sea. Someday I just know the *Bounty* will come home. When it does, I'll be waiting. 'Go away,' I'll shout, as the *Bounty* comes sailing up the bay. 'Go away! We are all out of money!'"

By March 2000, *Bounty* was permanently tied to the pier in Fall River, in terrible shape. She was now leaking like a sieve. Back in Nova Scotia, the *Lunenburg Progress Enterprise* reported alarming estimates that *Bounty* was taking in about two thousand litres (about five or six hundred gallons) of water every hour of every day. She was in a permanent state of sinking. Only the pumps kept her from hitting bottom.

The Tall Ship *Bounty* Foundation told the Fall River *Herald*

Bounty *at dock in Fall River.*

News that *Bounty* needed at least a million dollars for refit and repairs. The problem was, the foundation itself was sinking in a sea of debt. A marketing consultant was working on a pro bono basis, trying to find either corporate sponsors who would step up, or buyers to take her over.

In late May, the paper broke the story the town was expecting: *Bounty* was officially up for sale for the asking price of $1,533,000. In the sad shape she was in, who would buy her? Naturally, the yacht broker sounded optimistic. Many Fall River residents, worn down by the constant burden of endless and costly maintenance, were not hopeful. *Bounty*'s debts were now reckoned to be around $500,000 plus outstanding payments to vendors. The Tall Ship *Bounty* Foundation was disbanded in the summer. *Bounty* was a sad spectacle, listing at her dock, enough to make Lunenburg shipwrights roll in their graves.

Tuesday, December 12, 2000, almost did *Bounty* in for good. It was a cold winter morning, and the hundred-kilometre-an-hour wind gusts blew white caps on the water. Russell Guerriero, a volunteer from a group called "Friends of the *Bounty* Inc." put on his winter jacket and made his way down to Davol Street. He wanted to check on the ship that he and his friends admired so much. They were privately trying to raise dollars to keep her in town. When Guerriero reached the deserted pier at Heritage State Park, he was appalled at what he

The US Coast Guard was called to help save a sinking Bounty.

saw. In the buffeting wind, *Bounty* was being repeatedly slammed against the pier. Holes were being punched in her wooden hull.

Urgent word went out. Other volunteers were summoned. They tied emergency docking lines to *Bounty*, attempting to haul her out of danger. They scrambled on board the windswept decks. Someone dialled 911. The fire department sent help, as did the Coast Guard.

Eventually, a tug saved the day by pulling *Bounty* away from the pier. The volunteers temporarily patched the rough holes that had been dug into *Bounty*'s Douglas fir sides. Disaster had been averted. Jay Chatterton, another of the volunteers, was defiant. "As far as I'm concerned," he told the *Herald News*, "[*Bounty*] is not leaving Fall River."

Two months later, in February, 2001, *Bounty* found a buyer. Or rather, a buyer found her. Robert Hansen Jr., was a multimillionaire boat enthusiast. He had amassed his fortune through Islandaire, his New York-based air-conditioning business. Now, he was going to put his money to good use on something he loved: ships and the sea.

He was going to save *Bounty*, come hell or high water. There would be both.

CHAPTER 12
A New Beginning

This boat [Bounty] is a publicity magnet. Wherever we go, the cameras will follow, as well as the people.
                    — ROBERT E. HANSEN JR., FEBRUARY, 2001

By an odd twist of fate, Robert Hansen's interest in tall ships was kindled by a trip he had taken on another vessel built in Lunenburg, Nova Scotia: HMS *Rose*. *Rose* was another historical replica built by Smith and Rhuland — the same yard that had launched *Bounty* in 1960 and *Bluenose II* in 1963. Years later, in 2000, when Hansen heard that *Bounty* was for sale in Fall River, Massachusetts, his ears pricked up.

Hansen loved ships and boats and was an avid sailor. In *Bounty* he saw an opportunity, not just to save a unique and storied ship, but

Robert Hansen Jr., owner of Bounty.

also to make money doing it. Once restored, Hansen calculated that *Bounty* could be used for corporate events and charters. She could host Outward Bound-style team-building exercises. Corporations might pay to have their logos fly on *Bounty*'s flags and banners. There was the tall-ships circuit, which brought in big bucks for the shipowners. Plus, *Bounty* was a proven crowd-pleaser wherever she went. People would lay down their money to walk up the gangplank and to touch the giant, wooden ship's wheel that both Clark Gable and Marlon Brando had held. Ultimately, Hansen dreamed of sailing *Bounty* to Tahiti and the Pitcairn Islands. Captain Robin Walbridge couldn't believe his good luck. Finally, there was someone who believed in *Bounty* as much as he did.

In the meantime, there was just one problem: *Bounty* was in a desperate condition. Shortly after signing the owner's papers in September 2001, Hansen had his first taste of *Bounty* reality. In Fall River, the town's fire department and the Coast Guard had to act fast when *Bounty*'s bilge pumps failed and she started to sink at the dock. *Bounty* was taking on thousands of gallons an hour — the equivalent of an Olympic-sized swimming pool in a single day. It was time to start spending serious money, something which Hansen and his business partners were ready to do.

First, they made a makeshift covering for *Bounty*'s hull out of plastic, tarps and nailed-on sheets of plywood. A shipyard worker called it a "giant rubber diaper."

It may have lacked dignity, but at least it made it possible to tow *Bounty* out of Fall River. She made it to Gloucester, MA, but the shipyard there declined to work on her. So, they towed her farther up the coast to Sample's Shipyard in Boothbay Harbor, Maine. Sample's had a long history of building and repairing wooden ships, much like Lunenburg, Nova Scotia. The yard was equipped with the know-how for what promised to be a big repair job. *Bounty* was hauled out on the yard's marine railway.

The hull was in even worse shape than Walbridge and Hansen

Bounty in her new home of Greenport, New York.

had feared. Planks were warped and loose. Fasteners had corroded. The wood was tunnelled through by small, unshelled clams called Teredo worms — the marine equivalent of termites. Out came Hansen's chequebook, and the yard got to work. In this, the first of several refits *Bounty* would get in the next decade, the hull below the waterline was completely rebuilt, using all new wood.

After a job that lasted almost a year, *Bounty* was now at least seaworthy. Still, the US Coast Guard withheld the certification that Hansen was counting on. There would be no large groups of paying customers heading out to sea on *Bounty* anytime soon. *Bounty* was restricted to her status as a "moored attraction," which meant that — just as in Fall River — the public could only visit *Bounty* when she was safely tied up at a dock.

On July 26, 2002, Captain Robin Walbridge and Robert Hansen sailed *Bounty* to her new homeport of Greenport, New York, on the eastern tip of Long Island. The *New York Times* reported that a hundred people were on hand to take pictures and cheer her arrival. Walbridge spoke to the *Times* reporter. "I've got the greatest job in the world," he said. "This is not about saving a ship, it's about saving the skills. It's important we keep these skills alive so people remember how eighteenth-century square-riggers were sailed."

With their dreams of a "certified passenger vessel" unfulfilled, Hansen and Walbridge put *Bounty* to work. The HMS *Bounty* Foundation was created. As with many tall ships, *Bounty* was the centrepiece of a new non-profit organization. Annual operating costs came in at around $500,000, and no matter how many events and ports she visited, no matter how many admission tickets she sold, *Bounty* was hard-pressed to pay the bills. Hansen found himself digging deeper and deeper into his pockets, to the tune of millions of dollars.

When she wasn't on tour, *Bounty* occasionally resumed her old role of movie star. She appeared in the second and third installments of Walt Disney's *Pirates of the Caribbean* movie franchise. In 2004, *Bounty* appeared as Pirate Captain Pinty's ship in the movie version of *SpongeBob SquarePants.*

Her most notorious brush with the cameras happened in 2005. *Bounty* was wintering in her old home in St. Petersburg, FL, when a film production called *Pirates* came calling and rented *Bounty* as a location. The foundation was scandalized when the film was eventually released. It turned out *Pirates* was a hard-core pornographic film. *Bounty*'s Executive Director Margaret Ramsey had to handle the excited media calls. How had *Bounty* ended up in a porn film?

"There are people out there who don't have morals," said Ramsey to a newspaper reporter, adding without the slightest trace of irony, "It was supposed to be about Sinbad and a magic sceptre."

The inevitable jokes followed. There were references to "Swash and Unbuckling." *Bounty*'s organization was embarrassed. Hansen

Bounty *at sea.*

and Walbridge were not happy with the notoriety. The filmmakers were delighted.

In 2006, *Bounty* went back to Boothbay Harbor for another major, year-long overhaul and refit. This time, new decking was added, new windows and skylights, new stern and bow sections were built. Ballast was recast. The bill was a whopping $2 million. Hansen wrote another cheque.

Bounty looked good as she headed east, across the Atlantic for a publicity tour of the UK. There, the British tour organizer put out a news release saying *Bounty* appeared in two of the *Pirates of the Caribbean* films, portraying Johnny Depp's ship *Black Pearl*. Crowds flocked to see her. The cash registers rang and everything went fine until sharp-eyed, twelve-year-old Ross Winstanley from Devon cried foul. *Bounty* didn't look like *Black Pearl* at all, he told his mum. And *Bounty*'s tour-guiding crew had to agree.

"THE BLACK PEARL SHIP THAT'S JUST A FAKE!" blasted the headline in the *Daily Express*. Again, *Bounty*'s Executive Director Margaret Ramsey was put on the spot. It had all been a mistake. "I can only ask that people accept an apology," she said.

Mrs. Winstanley, having parted with £7.50 to see a ship that was merely a background performer in *Pirates of the Caribbean*, was inconsolable. "Ross is gutted," she told the *Express*.

Back in North America, *Bounty* became a regular on the tall-ships circuit. These are hugely popular events in seaport communities on both coasts of North America and Europe. Money is raised through corporate and government sponsorship, and a fee is paid to each visiting tall ship. In addition, ship organizations receive money from the paying public, who open their wallets for an opportunity to visit the ships in port. Tall-ship festivals have become an important part of the annual incomes of the non-profits who own the ships.

Hansen, Walbridge and the HMS *Bounty* Foundation were active participants. But *Bounty* always seemed a little apart from the other, better-funded organizations. People in the tall-ship community knew that *Bounty* had maintenance issues. They knew she was a leaky ship. They knew that the classification "moored attraction" meant that *Bounty* was not entirely up to snuff. In quiet conversations, people who knew about *Bounty*'s overall condition were concerned. Notwithstanding, there was admiration for Robin Walbridge, who had never given up on the ship he loved. And now — with a new owner investing money in upgrades — the general

Bounty at the dock beside the Fisheries Museum of the Atlantic in Lunenburg, 2012.

sense was that *Bounty* was slowly but surely on the rebound, closer to shipshape than she had been for years.

Less well-known was that Hansen had started to look around for a buyer. In 2010, he put her up for sale, with an asking price of $4.6 million. For his part, Robin Walbridge was a realist. The two of them had failed to secure dependable revenues that covered the annual costs. Walbridge understood that Hansen's chequebook had its limits.

First it was MGM. Then Ted Turner. Then Fall River. Now it was the millionaire boat-lover from New York. For the fourth time in her life *Bounty* was considered a financial liability, something to be offloaded.

Bounty's last tall-ship tour in the summer of 2012 took her to Port Hawkesbury, Pictou, Shelburne and Halifax, where for many Nova Scotians she was the star attraction. In Lunenburg, the coastal

Boatbuilders Gerald Zwicker, Edward Mosher and Edgar Silver reunited aboard
Bounty *in Lunenburg, August 3, 2012.*

town where she had been crafted in 1960, the surviving builders
came on board to share memories with the crew, and to marvel at
what they had put together as young men.

Bounty's final refit at Boothbay Harbor happened in September
and October of 2012. The young *Bounty* crew helped as best they
could. New fuel and water tanks were installed. Some electrical
wiring was replaced. Inappropriately, household caulking from
a hardware store was used to fill in some cracks. Some topside
decking was replaced and work was done on the masts. All
necessary jobs. But during the month-long refit, a more serious
problem was found. Underneath the planking, some of the ship's
ribs were black with rot. Hansen and Walbridge were furious, since
those same ribs had been installed at Boothbay just a few years
before. The shipyard foreman recommended the rotting wood be
replaced, but Walbridge said no. He was on a schedule. He had
neither the time nor access to the funds for such a major repair. In

his opinion the problem could be dealt with during a subsequent refit. He instructed that the rot be painted over.

When *Bounty* was refloated on October 17, 2012, in preparation for her voyage down to Florida for the winter, she looked as good as she had in years. The looks were deceiving; *Bounty* motored out of Boothbay with a multitude of worrying issues. Her communications systems were acting up. Her all-important bilge pumps were not all in working order. Worst of all, despite the millions of dollars Hansen had invested in improvements, *Bounty* had structural weaknesses. Walbridge must have known, but his mostly inexperienced crew was oblivious.

Bounty set a course south, to a rendezvous in New London, Connecticut. As they went about their appointed tasks, the crew felt a chill in the October breeze. Thousands of nautical miles away, on the other side of the Atlantic, a heated desert wind was blowing off the coast of West Africa. As the wind headed west toward the Caribbean, it drew energy from the moist warm air rising from the water. In the Caribbean Sea, just south of Jamaica, it became a

Bounty *at Boothbay Harbor, ME, during her final refit in 2012.*

Some of Bounty's *devoted but mostly inexperienced 2012 crew, awaiting instructions.*

tropical depression, and then slowly organized itself into a tropical cyclone. No one knew it yet, but this weather system would become a catastrophic storm.

With seawater slowly seeping through her hull, *Bounty* chugged southwards. She was less than two weeks away from the most terrifying episode of her storied career.

It would be her final chapter.

Two people on board would not live to tell the tale.

CHAPTER 13
Into the Hurricane

Out on the open ocean in a boat, under sail. The boat is moving, the wind tends to be quiet. You've got stars or sky, and sea. It's just a lovely place to be. It's a lot like being in love.

— DOUG FAUNT, *BOUNTY* CREW MEMBER

Tall-ship crew members are not your average citizens. They forgo the creature comforts of life ashore in exchange for the taste of travel and adventure at sea. They are not in it for the money, because usually there isn't much pay involved. "Volunteers who get beer money," is how *Bounty* Captain Robin Walbridge once described them. They tend to be younger men and women with an independent streak, individuals looking for life lessons in resilience and resourcefulness. How much they learn and how they learn it has a lot to do with the ship they crew on, and on the command structure in place. The crew quickly learns the meaning of inter-dependence, since few things on a tall ship can be accomplished by working alone. Weighing anchor, setting or furling sails, maintenance and repairs, sailing the vessel, safety drills — all these things require organized teamwork. Special bonds and meaningful friendships are developed on board a ship. Canoodling is not unheard of. Loyalty to fellow crew members, to the ship and to the captain is paramount.

In the fall of 2012, *Bounty* had a predominantly young crew. Half of them were in their twenties with limited experience at sea. For many of them, *Bounty* was the only tall ship they knew. They had a love of the ship and a fierce loyalty to Walbridge. He was their father figure, their instructor and their protector. They would follow him anywhere, up to and including the very brink of disaster.

October 25, 2012, was a long day for *Bounty*'s fifteen-person crew. In New London, CT, they had spent most of the day on a goodwill visit with a US Navy crew from the nearby submarine base. Walbridge and some of the crew leaders were keeping a weather eye on a large storm that had brewed up in the Caribbean and was heading north. Like all hurricanes, this one was given a name: Sandy. Marine forecasts were unambiguous about it. This storm was big and getting bigger. It would bring with it hurricane-force winds; it would in all likelihood cause massive destruction. Potentially, it would kill. Worryingly, the projected track of Sandy brought it up the eastern seaboard, possibly to New England, where *Bounty* was now tied up.

Shortly after 5 p.m., First Mate John Svendsen had a private conversation with Walbridge, urging him to seek safe refuge further inland, or in other nearby, more protected harbours. Walbridge had a different idea, one that would get *Bounty* down to her old home in St. Petersburg, FL, on schedule. St. Pete's was also where Walbridge lived, and where his wife was eagerly awaiting his return. Today was his sixty-third birthday.

NASA satellite image of the northern hemisphere, showing the size of Hurricane Sandy.

Captain Robin Walbridge in his Bounty *cabin.*

Shortly after his conversation with Svendsen, Walbridge called a meeting of all hands. *Bounty*'s crew regularly had meetings at the capstan — a large, wooden, spool-shaped piece of winch gear on deck, near the stern. The crew gathered around. Walbridge told them that he planned to set sail very shortly; that they may have heard about a big storm coming their way, but they shouldn't worry about it. *Bounty* had survived bad weather before, even hurricanes, and she'd be fine again this time. The crew listened intently. Some of them had already heard from immediate family members, who had relayed news reports about the storm. A "Frankenstorm" was how some news reports were describing it.

Walbridge told the crew that a ship was safer at sea than tied to a dock, where it could be battered to pieces. He told them he had a plan to sail around the storm, that all would be well. Then, he offered up a dramatic option: anyone wanting to leave the ship could do so right then and there, no hard feelings. New London's Amtrak station was just down the road. No travelling expenses were offered up. First Mate Svendsen said nothing at the meeting, not wanting to question — and thereby undermine — his captain.

"I've got to say one of my thoughts was, 'That's pretty sudden.' It would be a little hard to get off the boat in a hurry on this short notice," remembers the ship's electrician, Able Seaman Doug Faunt.

Faunt was one of *Bounty*'s veterans. A sixty-six-year-old, financially secure retiree from California, he had joined *Bounty* in 2008. Some of the younger crew members looked at the experienced hands for cues. No one took Walbridge up on his offer to get off the ship.

"We had a short crew. If anyone did get off, then we'd be an even shorter crew," said Faunt.

Doug Faunt, Bounty's *volunteer electrician.*

Bounty *deckhands at work.*

The impulse to stick together — to face whatever was coming as a united crew — won out. On the one day when arguably there should have been a mutiny on Lunenburg's *Bounty,* there wasn't even discussion or dissent. The crew got busy with preparations for departure.

Bounty slid quietly out of New London soon afterward, on a clear evening with calm seas. Apart from Walbridge, Svendsen and a few of the older hands, most of the crew had no idea what it would be like to be aboard *Bounty* in a storm. The ship's engineer, Chris Barksdale, was a fifty-six-year-old mechanic and handyman who had just joined *Bounty* weeks before, during the Boothbay Harbor refit. This was his first real passage on his very first ship. Deckhand Jessica Hewitt, twenty-five years old, had been with *Bounty* all of

Joshua Scornavacchi, Bounty *crewmember, 2012.*

two months. Twenty-five-year-old Joshua Scornavacchi — a self-described "adrenalin junkie" — had been a deckhand for just seven months. In all, of the sixteen crew members on *Bounty,* no fewer than nine had joined the ship in 2012. The cook, thirty-four-year-old Jessica Black, had joined *Bounty*'s crew *that very day.*

Of all the new crew members, possibly the most enthusiastic was an engaging and gregarious forty-one-year-old American named Claudene Christian.

"Claudene Christian was a little fireball of energy and passion," says Scornavacchi. "When she came on the boat everyone was pretty shocked, because she showed up wearing all pink and white, not much like a tall-ship sailor, almost the opposite in fact. But she had a passion that a lot of people don't have. That was very attractive and led everybody to kind of just fall in love with her as a person."

Before volunteering to crew on *Bounty* in May 2012, Claudene Christian had no crewing experience whatever. She did, however, claim a very special connection to *Bounty.* She had been told by her uncle that her branch of the Christian family tree had connections to

Claudene Christian, who joined Bounty's *crew in May 2012.*

the Isle of Man, UK, where Fletcher Christian's family hailed from hundreds of years earlier. Doing the generational math, Claudene told everyone she was the great-great-great-great-granddaughter of *Bounty's* original mutineer. The claim is unproven, and probably mistaken, but she believed it, and that's what counted to her. It was a neat story. No one on *Bounty* took issue with it.

As they prepared the ship for bad weather, securing everything on deck, Christian and the other crew members were unaware of just how massive a storm Sandy had become. It was almost 1,500 kilometres (900 miles) wide. Walbridge had told the crew they would sail east — as far east as Newfoundland if need be — to sail around Sandy. But that's not what happened.

During his watch at the helm, Doug Faunt knew something was up. "We were headed south," Faunt recalls. "I was like 'Why are we headed south? Shouldn't we be headed east?' But I was doing what I was told."

Claudine texted her mother: "I love you mom and dad. Don't worry it will be fine. Our captain has thirty years experience and

Claudene Christian at Bounty's *helm.*

our ship is strong. They say *Bounty* loves hurricanes."

Claudine's mother texted back: "We love you so much! Please be careful!"

Claudine's response took an odd turn: "Just be sure that I am okay. HAPPY TO BE HERE on *Bounty* . . . doing what I love. And if I do go down with the ship and the worst happens just know that I am TRULY GENUINELY HAPPY!!! And I am doing what I love! I love you."

By Friday, October 26, 2012, *Bounty* was 150 nautical miles off the New Jersey coast, an increasingly lonely blip on the radar. She was travelling fast, enjoying a following wind with the sails up and both diesel engines pushing hard. Most shipping — including the US Navy — was getting out of Sandy's path. Up and down the coast, vessels of all sizes were seeking shelter in places such as New Bedford, the Delaware Bay, the Upper Chesapeake, Baltimore or up the Hudson River. In Lunenburg, Nova Scotia, the captain of the *Picton Castle* studied the weather forecasts and delayed a planned departure. Walbridge was unfazed and pressed on. He sent regular email updates to HMS *Bounty*'s office in New York, which in turn fed him the latest information on the storm. Walbridge showed no signs of concern at all.

By Saturday, October 27, the destructive power of Sandy had become evident and was being widely reported. Parts of Jamaica

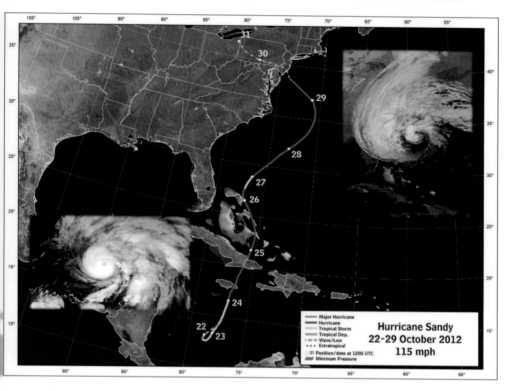

The track of Hurricane Sandy.

had been left devastated. Flooding in Haiti had killed fifty-four people and left two hundred thousand people homeless. Deaths were reported in the Dominican Republic and Cuba. The Bahamas were hit hard. In the southeastern US, flights and trains were being cancelled. Tropical storm watches were being declared in states from Florida to New England. President Barak Obama signed emergency declarations. The National Guard was put on alert. This was the real deal. A gargantuan hurricane, on a collision course with two other weather systems.

Bounty's Facebook page lit up with messages expressing deep concern that she was out at sea.

"*That they'd choose to take this risk is criminal,*" read one.

From his home, the father of twenty-nine-year-old deckhand Drew Salapatek pushed back on Facebook: "*Rest assured that the*

Bounty is safe and in very capable hands. Bounty's current voyage is a calculated decision . . . NOT AT ALL . . . irresponsible or with a lack of foresight as some have suggested. The fact of the matter is . . . A SHIP IS SAFER AT SEA THAN IN PORT!"

Not this time. *Bounty* was far from safe. By this point, one of her two main generators was acting up and had to be shut down. The bilge pumps were having trouble keeping up with the water coming in. The sea state grew worse, and *Bounty* started to heave and roll in ten-foot swells. Chris Barksdale, the rookie engineer, took a bad fall and seriously injured his hand. The crew was exhausted. The galley was becoming a dangerous place to be, and Jessica Black wasn't able to prepare proper meals. Crewmembers were getting seasick. The situation was worsening by the hour. No call of any kind was made to alert the US Coast Guard that *Bounty* was at sea and might need monitoring.

Rough weather off Bounty's *starboard side.*

Rough weather recorded by a Bounty *crewman.*

Sometime early on Saturday afternoon, Walbridge took a decision to alter course. Based on the reports he was getting, it seemed to him that Sandy was veering east, away from the coast. His best plan, he concluded, was to head southwest — essentially to squeeze between Sandy and the coast. He also knew that with the counterclockwise rotation of a hurricane, and his calculation that he'd end up in the equivalent of the eleven o'clock position, *Bounty* would get one hell of a ride, with the following hurricane wind pushing her southwards toward her destination.

Walbridge's plan was based on an educated guess, no more. Superstorm Sandy wobbled, changed direction, and started to head north again. There would be no room for *Bounty* to squeeze between Sandy and the coastline. *Bounty* was heading straight toward the bared teeth of a monster.

Bounty *heeling over in high winds.*

By Saturday night, it was clear to all the officers on board that their ship was in distress. Still Walbridge would not order a call to the Coast Guard. During the night, the crew quarters became soaked with seawater. Sleeping was impossible. With the ship's rookie engineer injured and seriously seasick, Walbridge himself spent more and more time trying to fix the bilge pumps in the engine room, a sure sign the ship was in big trouble.

By first light on Sunday morning October 28, 2012, *Bounty* was flooding. This would have been the time to start preparations to abandon ship and to initiate an SOS call. Captain Walbridge refused. Midmorning, *Bounty* was hit by a huge wave and Walbridge was sent flying through the air, taking what Barksdale called a "huge fall," landing hard on his back. To add to all the other problems, now *Bounty*'s skipper was seriously hurt.

Throughout the day on Sunday, system after system started to fail: generators, pumps, engines and instruments. Waves smashed a window in the Great Cabin, and water poured in. *Bounty* was taking a beating, and so were the crew. It was now a full-time job in the hot engine room — where working conditions were appalling — just to keep the pumps working at all. The water level was rising steadily. At 3:30 p.m., First Mate Svendsen asked Walbridge to call the Coast Guard. Again, Walbridge said no. At 5:30 p.m., twenty-nine-year-old Adam Prokosh was slammed against a bulkhead, injuring his head, breaking ribs and possibly his spine. Claudene Christian tended to him as best she could, propping him up in a corner on a mattress.

Even then — no distress call from *Bounty*.

Bounty was in a situation that just kept deteriorating: seams in the ship were opening up from the torque of the waves against the hull, and more water was coming in than could be pumped out; electrical systems were shutting down, on and off plunging *Bounty* into total darkness; the crew was cold and exhausted, literally hanging on to whatever was at hand so that they didn't fall and get hurt; fuel was leaking in the engine room; the communications systems were becoming unreliable; people were getting electric shocks where sea water was hitting electrical connections; the sound and fury of the storm was upon them; and yet — incredibly — no one off the ship knew that any of this was going on.

Eventually, at 8:30 p.m. that evening, Walbridge relented. *Bounty* made what is known as a "pan-pan" call to the Coast Guard. A pan-pan call is meant to signify that there is a "safety situation" of some urgency on board a vessel. The Coast Guard logged *Bounty*'s call, followed protocol and inferred that *Bounty* and the souls on board were in no immediate danger. Had *Bounty* sent out a "Mayday" call the Coast Guard's reaction would have been immediate and very different.

At 10:15 p.m., with the hurricane raging around his ship and radio communications no longer working, Walbridge sent an email to *Bounty* headquarters:

> *We are taking on water. We will probably need assistance in the morning. SAT* [satellite] *phone not working very good. We have activated the EPIRB* [emergency locator beacon]. *We are not in danger tonight, but if conditions don't improve on the boat we will be in Danger tomorrow. . . . The boat is doing great, we can't de-water.*

Marine experts and ship captains have long pondered what on earth Walbridge could have meant by "The boat is doing great . . ." because by any standards it clearly wasn't.

Fifteen minutes after the first email, at 10:30 p.m., Walbridge sent another email:

> *My first guess was that we had until morning before we have to abandon. Seeing the water rise I am not sure we have that long. We have activated our EPIRB.*

Bounty was sinking, and everybody on board now knew it. There could be no more denials. This was really happening, in the worst place, at the worst possible time. *Bounty*'s age had finally caught up to her. The years of cutting corners, of not having the funds to properly rebuild, of living life on the fringe of the tall-ship community, of taking a "moored attraction" out to sea — all were coalescing into an unfolding catastrophe, in the darkness of a raging tempest.

Bounty crew member Doug Faunt would later put it this way: "We'd been living so close to the edge for so long that we were used to being out there on the edge. All of a sudden, the edge disappeared."

Bounty, *pushed onto her beam ends in the storm.*

CHAPTER 14
Lost at Sea

The only thing I could think of was "Did I just promise my mom and my little brother that I wasn't going to die?" And now, that's exactly what I was doing. I was dying and I couldn't do anything about it. Then I broke the surface and I was able to take a breath.

— JOSHUA SCORNAVACCHI, *BOUNTY* CREW MEMBER

One of the first things people will tell you about being on a ship in a hurricane is the incredible noise. It is the loudest howling of wind you can imagine, accompanied by a deep thundering frequency, like a passing train. On deck, conversation is virtually impossible. To be heard, you have to get very close to the other person, face to face, mere inches apart, and you bellow at the top of your lungs. Maybe, just maybe, you'll be understood. Now, imagine doing this while being pelted with heavy rain that hits your face so hard it actually hurts. You can't keep your eyes open. You're standing on a slippery wooden deck that is heaving constantly — up thirty feet into the air, and then down again. Repeatedly. It feels like your stomach is in your mouth. The ship is listing badly to one side. If you don't hold onto something solid, and maintain a white-knuckle grip, you will surely fall, slide very fast, and slam into something hard that will likely break a bone. It is a terrifying experience, and no one who has lived through it wants to repeat it.

At 1 a.m. on Monday, October 29, 2012, these were the conditions faced by the sixteen men and women aboard *Bounty*. The ship was located some ninety nautical miles off Cape Hatteras, NC. At the best of times, it's a hazardous place for sailors. The cold Labrador Current hits the northbound warm waters of the Gulf Stream. The sea is notoriously turbulent, and the currents are treacherous. The ocean floor is littered with shipwrecks. It's called the Graveyard of the Atlantic, and it might just be the worst place on the planet to get caught in a hurricane.

Bounty was filling with water and was surely going to sink. Sooner or later, the crew were going to have to climb over the side in total darkness, and take their chances in the black, mountainous waves.

Fifty nautical miles away, a US Coast Guard HC-130J Hercules plane from Elizabeth City's Air Station was plowing through violent turbulence, heading toward the signal emanating from *Bounty*'s emergency locator beacon. Even with their green night-vision goggles on, the pilots could see almost nothing ahead except thick bands of cloud and torrents of rain. In the back of the plane, the flight technicians were vomiting uncontrollably from motion sickness. The flight deck placed a radio call to *Bounty*.

Inside *Bounty*'s navigation cabin, First Mate John Svendsen heard the C-130 and responded. He gave the ship's position and

US Coast Guard HC-130J at Elizabeth City, North Carolina.

US Coast Guard Jayhawk helicopter at Elizabeth City, North Carolina.

status. Sixteen souls on board. Both generators failed. No engines. No pumps. Dwindling battery power on the hand-held radio. The pilots reduced altitude and swooped in for a closer look. With their night-vision goggles, they spotted a beam of light coming through the murk. Someone on *Bounty* was pointing a flashlight at the plane.

Descending as low over the wave tops as they dared, co-pilot Mike Myers suddenly exclaimed that he saw something.

"What is it? What do you see?" asked the pilot, Wes McIntosh.

Myers: "I see a giant pirate ship in the middle of a hurricane."

On board *Bounty*, the crew was gathering anything they thought would be useful when they abandoned ship. The life rafts were getting readied. Walbridge still held out hope that somehow the Coast Guard was going to be able to drop pumps down to *Bounty* as they had in 1998, that by some miracle the ship could be saved again. The wind and sea conditions made that impossible. The C-130 crew alerted Elizabeth City that Coast Guard helicopters had to be dispatched, so that any survivors could be winched up from the water. As they roared over *Bounty*'s masts, just five hundred feet in the air, the Hercules flight mechanics dropped flares, a self-locating marker buoy and two inflatable life rafts.

At 3 a.m., Walbridge, now defeated but ever the instructor, asked the crew members clustered around him: "What went wrong? At what point did we lose control?" It was largely a rhetorical question. By this point, the crew was more focused on survival.

In a last-ditch attempt at saving the ship, some of the crew attempted to start up what's known as a "trash pump," essentially a small, gasoline-powered water pump that can be bought in any hardware store. It had never been tested on *Bounty* since the day it was purchased. Barksdale, the ship's stricken engineer, didn't even know it was on board. No matter. It wouldn't start now. Following orders, the crew began to climb into their "Gumby suits," bulky red neoprene survival suits, with large attached boots and hoods. At about 3:30 a.m., Svendsen advised Walbridge it was time to launch the life rafts and abandon ship. Walbridge balked, certain they had more time, with luck until daybreak. Another bad call, as subsequent events would prove.

For the next hour, the crew hung on for their lives as *Bounty* groaned and rolled in towering thirty-foot seas. Seams in the hull opened up. Water rose higher inside the hull. The crew tried to reassure each other as best they could. There was no panic.

Scornavacchi remembers an encounter with Christian. "Claudene came up, and she sat beside me, and she looked up at me and smiled. And she made her face scrunch up, which is like her 'determined' face."

The C-130 flew overhead, monitoring the situation, talking to First Mate Svendsen on the hand-held radio, feeding updated information back to the incoming Coast Guard Jayhawk helicopter.

At 4:35 a.m., Svendsen would wait no longer. "It's time to go!" he yelled out into the roaring gale. Everyone knew what this meant. Time to launch the life rafts and abandon ship. No sooner had the words left Svendsen's mouth than *Bounty* was swamped by a huge ocean wave and was pushed over onto her side. Crew members were hurled into the water, individually and in small groups. It was utter chaos. With *Bounty* on her starboard side, her masts now lay across the wave tops. The sea water around the hull was churning furiously with immersed deck gear, miles of heavy ropes and rigging. Struggling to stay afloat and gasping for air, some of the crew members were struck by falling debris. Some got caught up in rope lines that spooled out under the surface. As waves pushed *Bounty* up, her masts rose up off the surface, high into the air. In the wave trough, the masts and rigging came smashing down on top of the struggling crew.

Doug Faunt: "I got pushed underwater a couple of times. I thought that I was going to get tangled in the rigging, and the thought that went through my head was this is a stupid way to die."

"I was pretty mad," says Scornavacchi. "I was angry because that wasn't part of the plan. I felt like we should be in rafts. We shouldn't have fallen in the water. This doesn't make any sense. Why is this happening?"

"I knew there were people around me," Faunt says. "But it was basically a swim-for-your-life situation. I looked for other people, but I couldn't see anybody in that environment."

Ninety nautical miles away, back at the Coast Guard station in Elizabeth City, word spread fast. "They're in the water." A second Jayhawk helicopter took off, powering headlong into Sandy's furious bands of wind and rain.

Bounty was now mostly submerged. To survive, the crew had to get away from the ship and its lethal thrashing. Helped by moonlight, small groups of survivors started to locate each other. With enormous difficulty, weighed down by seawater sloshing around in their Gumby suits, they helped each other into drifting life rafts. There was no way of knowing who was where. Some people were missing. As the hours dragged by, and the Hercules circled overhead, it started to sink in to *Bounty*'s exhausted crew.

US Coast Guard helicopter lowering a rescue swimmer.

We have lost the ship. Occasionally a large wave would smack the life raft, causing it to "clam-shell." The raft would be violently folded in half. People inside were smashed into each other. Even now, in the relative safety of the raft, people were getting hurt.

The first Coast Guard Jayhawk helicopter arrived on scene at 6:40 a.m., around first light. A short distance from *Bounty*, the First Mate Svendsen was spotted floating alone in his survival suit. His strobe light blinked white against the dark sea. A rescue swimmer was lowered into the water, as the chopper pilots struggled to keep the aircraft steady, nose to the wind.

Svendsen was grabbed, put in a rescue basket, and winched

US Coast Guard helicopter lifting a rescue swimmer and a survivor.

aboard. Next, the helicopter hovered over an inflated life raft. The rescue swimmer helped crew members clamber out. One by one, they were winched up to safety.

The second Jayhawk arrived and maneuvered over a different life raft. The pilots could see faces poking through the flapped door

US Coast Guard Flight Mechanic Gregory Moulder.

of the raft, looking up at them. In the back of the helicopter, flight mechanic Gregory Moulder checked the safety harness and sling of his rescue swimmer Dan Todd. Moulder muscled the helicopter's sliding side door open.

"I opened the door and all I saw were huge waves," says Moulder. "Just huge white caps and rolling seas. I was just in awe. It was raining up on me, it was raining down on me. It was coming in from the side, from everywhere."

In the helicopter cockpit, the pilots were drawing on every ounce of their flying experience. The flight commander's main job is to keep the helicopter level and hovering over the targets in the water.

Twenty-seven-year-old Jenny Fields was in the co-pilot seat. Her job was to maintain what is known on the flight deck as "situational awareness." She had to monitor fuel level and remaining flying time. She had to communicate with the C-130 circling overhead. She had to monitor the aircraft's clearance above the constantly fluctuating

US Coast Guard helicopter pilot Jenny Fields.

wave crests, alerting the aircraft commander and the flight mechanic about incoming swells. She had to calculate the flight plan back to base. And she had to do all these things concurrently *in the midst of a hurricane.*

On-board cameras recorded that morning's Coast Guard's rescue operation. The extraordinary footage is still posted on YouTube. When the automated warning chirps out "Altitude . . . Altitude . . ." the helicopter is just twenty feet above the tops of the waves.

When all the survivors were loaded onto the two helicopters, the Jayhawks began a rough two-hour flight back to base, buffeted by brutal headwinds. No one could talk much above the din of the engines, but some of *Bounty*'s crew did the math and they became concerned that two crewmembers were missing.

In the grey light of morning, October 29, 2012, the helicopters landed in Elizabeth City. The survivors, still in their Gumby suits, were helped across the tarmac and into the hanger. Newscasts

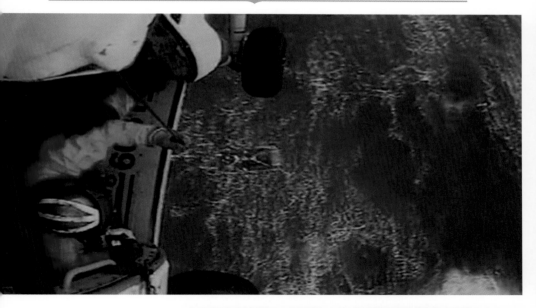

Top: *A helicopter-mounted camera shows a flight mechanic raising a* Bounty *survivor in a rescue basket.*

Right: *US Coast Guard footage of a* Bounty *life raft.*

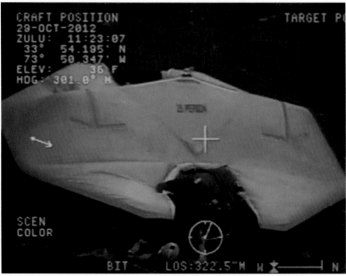

CRAFT POSITION
29-OCT-2012
ZULU: 11:23:07
  33° 54.195' N
  73° 50.347' W
ELEV: 36 F
HDG: 301.0° M

TARGET P

SCEN
COLOR

BIT   LOS:322.5°M W⚓———I N

updated the extraordinary rescue story. Up and down the coast people were wondering: What on earth was *Bounty* doing out there in the first place?

The survivor head count was made official. Two of *Bounty's* sixteen men and women were in fact missing.

Later that afternoon, the Coast Guard located Claudene Christian floating face down in her survival suit, seven nautical

Bounty survivors arrive at Elizabeth City, North Carolina.

miles from *Bounty*'s last reported position. She had a cut on her nose, as if she had been struck by something. She was unresponsive. Non-stop attempts at CPR all the way back to Elizabeth City made no difference. Claudene — the ever-smiling and most enthusiastic among *Bounty*'s new 2012 crew — was dead.

Captain Robin Walbridge was still missing. He was last seen on deck, his survival suit only half on, hugging his hips. He was heading for the stern, just as *Bounty* tipped over. A third Coast Guard helicopter flew out to the site to search for him. The flight crew captured the very last pictures ever taken of *Bounty*.

In her lifetime, *Bounty* had been filmed and photographed literally millions of times. But never like this. She was sitting completely alone in a white-capped sea, her interior flooded, listing badly to port, her decks awash. No one could help her now. It was only a matter of time. Early Monday evening, a Coast Guard cutter observed *Bounty* lying on her side. Some time after that, in the dark with no one to bear witness, she slipped beneath the surface, and began a slow descent, fourteen thousand feet to the seabed below.

Still pressed between the mainmast and her original keel —
the good luck silver dollar placed there fifty-two years before, in
Lunenburg, Nova Scotia.

The Coast Guard kept looking for Walbridge. The search lasted
four days, covering some ten thousand overlapping nautical square
miles. His body was never found.

Top: Bounty *sinking on
October 29, 2012.*

Left: *Infrared image of*
Bounty *shortly before
she sinks to the bottom.*

Epilogue

History isn't just the story of bad people doing bad things. It's quite as much a story of people trying to do good things. But somehow, something goes wrong.

— C. S. LEWIS, *MERE CHRISTIANITY* (1952)

The big questions about *Bounty*'s sinking in Hurricane Sandy are the same today as they were in October 2012: Why did it have to happen at all? What was *Bounty* doing out there? What were the factors Robin Walbridge was weighing when he decided to cast off and head out to sea, with a hurricane churning its way up the Atlantic seaboard? The full story may never be known, but there are some things that are certain.

Bounty *sinking in 2012.*

Robin Walbridge and his wife Claudia McCann at Bounty's *wheel.*

Walbridge was not intimidated by the prospect of commanding *Bounty* in a hurricane. He'd done it before. In fact, he spoke openly about it in a television interview done earlier that summer during a stopover in Belfast, Maine.

"We chase hurricanes," Walbridge told the reporter. "You try and get up as close to the eye of it as you can. You stay down in the southeast quadrant . . . you don't want to get in front of it, but you'll get a good ride out of a hurricane."

We know that Walbridge had an appointment he wanted to keep in Florida, one that might have put badly needed dollars in *Bounty*'s bank account. An organization that promoted the needs of children with Down syndrome had expressed interest in partnering with *Bounty*, to create an on-board educational and developmental program for the kids. The meeting with the Ashley DeRamus

Foundation was set for November 9, 2012, in St. Petersburg. Could the prospect of financial salvation have been a factor?

With decades of experience, Walbridge expressed great confidence in being able to navigate around Sandy, outlining different strategies at different times to the crew and to *Bounty*'s headquarters in New York: "east around" (the storm) was one, squeezing between the west side of the storm and the coast was another.

In the end, none of it made any sense to anyone, sailors or landlubbers, and especially not to the tall-ship community, which was united in condemnation of Walbridge's decision to sail.

In February 2013, in Portsmouth, VA, the US Coast Guard and the National Transportation Safety Board (NTSB) conducted a joint inquiry into the sinking. Most of the crew testified, as did rescuers, ship captains and the project manager from Boothbay Harbor, Maine. What emerged during the testimony was a catalogue of hair-raising revelations about a ship that was short-crewed, that was known to have rot in her frames, that leaked badly, whose pumps were suspect at the very beginning of the journey, whose communications systems were untested before departure . . . on and on it went for nine days.

Bounty's owner, Robert Hansen, Jr., attended the hearings, but elected not to testify, invoking his Fifth Amendment rights. The Christian family had filed a $90 million lawsuit against Hansen and the HMS *Bounty* Organization LLC. Hansen was under no obligation to say anything that might incriminate himself.

Testifying at the inquiry, *Bounty*'s crew defended their captain at every opportunity. No one broke ranks. Their loyalty to Walbridge never wavered.

The NTSB report was officially released almost a year later, and it pulled no punches. "The probable cause of the sinking," stated the report, "was the captain's reckless decision to sail the vessel into the well-forecasted path of Hurricane Sandy, which subjected the

ADDENDUM:
The Other *Bounty*

For the past ten years, there has been another *Bounty* sailing on the South China Sea. A replica of HMAV *Bounty* was built for yet another movie version of the mutiny story. This 1984 film — *The Bounty*— starred Sir Anthony Hopkins (as William Bligh) and Mel Gibson (as Fletcher Christian). The cast also included Sir Laurence Olivier, Daniel Day-Lewis, Edward Fox and Liam Neeson. Just as MGM had done in 1960, the filmmakers decided to commission the building of a replica of *Bounty*, based on the original plans. The ship was built in Whangarei, New Zealand, in 1978–79, using materials gathered from all over the Commonwealth, including Canadian pine for the masts and yardarms.

After filming was completed, this version of *Bounty* was refitted in Vancouver, BC, sailed to the UK, and from there to Australia to take part in the First Fleet Re-enactment Voyage — part of the celebration of Australia's Bicentennial.

After serving as a tourist attraction in Sydney Harbour for two decades, she was sold to HKR International Limited in Hong Kong in 2007. There, she became one of the lures at a major resort complex named Discovery Bay. "The only European Tall Ship in Hong Kong," her owners trumpeted on the resort's website. *Bounty* was available for harbour cruises, charters, day excursions, weddings and corporate retreats.

With no fanfare or explanation, the operators of Discovery Bay announced on their website that this South Seas version of *Bounty* was decommissioned in September 2017.

Despite being completed on time and on budget, the 1984 film *The Bounty* was a money-loser at the box office. In common with all the earlier films, this version of the story had its fair share of historical inaccuracies, but it is widely regarded as the most accurate of all the movie versions. The friendship between Bligh and Christian is central to this adaptation, and Hopkins's portrayal of Captain William Bligh is nuanced — not at all like the sadist popularized by Charles Laughton in 1935. For his part, Mel Gibson thought that the film went too easy on Fletcher Christian, and that Christian — not Bligh — is the real villain of the *Bounty* story. William Bligh himself, who eventually retired from the British Navy in 1814 with the rank of vice-admiral, would surely have agreed.

Further Reading

In addition to the accounts mentioned in chapter 5, there are literally dozens of in-depth books about HMAV *Bounty* and the mutiny. To choose just one, I recommend *The Bounty: The True Story of the Mutiny on the Bounty* by Caroline Alexander. It is an extraordinarily detailed work of historical research and writing and does a brilliant job of filling in gaps and exploding myths — a masterpiece.

Captain Bligh and Mr. Christian: The Men and the Mutiny by Richard Hough is a wonderful read that undoes the Bligh-as-sadistic-tyrant myth perpetuated in Nordoff and Hall's earlier novels. Hough's telling of the *Bounty* story was used as the basis for the 1984 film version, widely regarded as the most nuanced portrayal of the two antagonists and their inevitable clash.

Anyone interested in the minutiae of HMAV *Bounty*'s construction will appreciate John McKay's *Anatomy of the Ship: The Armed Transport Bounty*, which contains a wealth of precise and detailed drawings.

Among the excellent accounts of events in 2012, three stand out: *The Sinking of the Bounty: The True Story of a Tragic Shipwreck and its Aftermath* by Matthew Shaer; *The Gathering Wind: Hurricane Sandy, the Sailing Ship* Bounty, *and a Courageous Rescue at Sea* by Gregory A. Freeman; and *Rescue of the Bounty: Disaster and Survival in Superstorm Sandy* by Michael J. Tougias and Douglas Campbell.

CNN Interactive has a thorough and well-researched account of the sinking. *Life and Death on the Bounty,* by Thom Patterson, is available online.

The online magazine gCaptain (gcaptain.com) provides detailed reporting of the sinking and the subsequent official inquiry.

For straight-up accounts of the events that led to the loss of *Bounty* in 2012, the official reports of the United States Coast Guard and the National Transportation Safety Board make interesting reading. Both are available online by searching *Bounty* on each organization's website: www.ntsb.gov and www.dco.uscg.mil

In its visual archives, CBC Television has preserved two documentaries worth watching: *Building the* Bounty (1960) and Bounty *in Tahiti* (1961). CBC also has an excellent *Land and Sea* episode (2001) about the Boothbay Harbor, ME, refit.

Many artifacts from the original *Bounty* have survived. Some are kept at the National Maritime Museum in Greenwich, UK. They include an eighteenth-century medical book, carefully bound in sailcloth, taken by one of the mutineers to Pitcairn; William Bligh's reading glass and clay pipe; the sea chest brought to Pitcairn by the longest-surviving mutineer John Adams; Peter Haywood's letters relating to the events surrounding the mutiny; pieces of *Bounty*'s rudder and copper sheathing; and, perhaps most oddly, John Adams's pigtail, mounted on black cloth in a gilded oval frame.

Acknowledgements

It takes a team of people to complete a book like this one, and I am indebted to many talented individuals along the way. Firstly, many thanks to Formac publisher Jim Lorimer for suggesting I should write it. Thanks to my friend Valerie Mansour who — after I had stared at a blank computer screen for about a week — told me decisively to "get on with it," to start anywhere, to just start writing. As simple as that may sound, it was actually tremendous advice. Thanks too for the expert and patient guidance of editor Kara Turner and editorial coordinator Heather Thomas, who were both gloriously unfazed by my lack of experience.

The story of the original eighteenth-century *Bounty* and her infamous mutiny has been told many times and in many forms since the actual events more than two hundred years ago. My own interest in the *Bounty* story began in 2013 with a television documentary about the fate of *Bounty*'s twentieth-century successor. The film *Bounty: Into the Hurricane* was commissioned by CBC Nova Scotia and produced by Tell Tale Productions. Many thanks to Peter Hall and Edward Peill, respectively, for the opportunity to write and direct that film. In making it, I interviewed modern-day *Bounty* crew members about life on board, and their near-death experience during Hurricane Sandy. I was also privileged to meet some of the heroes from the United States Coast Guard who risked their own lives to hoist *Bounty* survivors from a terrifying sea. As one of the rescued crew members put it: "They are angels come from the sky to save us. I had respect for them before. Now I have no words . . ."

I've been hooked on all things *Bounty* ever since.

Thanks are due to many generous organizations and individuals who made available the images used in the book. They include the Canadian Broadcasting Corporation, Fall River's *Herald News*, Claudene (Dina) Christian, Claudia McCann, Dwight Parker, Wray and Lois Dewar, and Tara Bearsley. Also, special thanks to Adrian Morrison, Devyn Kaizer and the rest of the helpful staff of the Nova Scotia Museum. This page is also an opportunity to pay tribute to a former CBC colleague: archivist and visual librarian Doug Kirby. By example, Doug taught the importance of preserving heritage, and the value of expressing our culture through storytelling. He is largely responsible for the brilliantly preserved archive of CBC programming, which to my endless gratitude includes several hours of footage about *Bounty*. My only regret is that Doug is no longer with us to witness his contribution to this book.

And finally, I want to thank my wife Kathy Sadoway and our two daughters Emma and Alice, who have always been unfailingly supportive of whatever I have tried to accomplish. To them, and everyone else who offered encouragement, advice or assistance: my sincere gratitude.

Geoff D'Eon

Halifax, Nova Scotia, 2018

Photo Credits

Adventist Digital Library: 92, 93

Alamy: 28

Boyd Family: 69

Canadian Broadcasting Company: 61, 76, 84

CBC Television: 109

City of Vancouver Archives: 79

Claudene Christian: 118, 123, 125, 126, 150

Claudia McCann: 121, 147

claymoreexpeditions.com: 46

Dixon Library, State Library of New South Wales: 45

Eddie Shamie: 88

Eric Browdy Hernandez: 115

Fall River Herald News: 98, 99, 100, 101, 102, 105, 106, 107, 113, 152

Fisheries Museum of The Atlantic: 60, 62, 63, 64, 65, 86, 87

Flickr, user aafes49: 30

Geoff D'Eon: 8, 9, 10, 11, 13, 141, 142

George Cruickshank: 18

Hampshire County Council Fine Art Collection: 22

HMS *Bounty* Foundation: 77, 96, 110

John Cleveley The Younger: 26

Lance Douglas: 117

Life Magazine: 78

Little Brown and Company USA: 53

Marc Castells: 128, 129, 130, 133

marinas.com: 58

Melva Warren Evans: 47

MGM: 50, 54, 55, 57, 82, 83, 94

NASA: 31, 120

National Gallery of Australia: 17, 39

National Geographic: 71

National Library of Australia: 37

National Maritime Museum, UK: 20, 24, 52

National Oceanic and Atmospheric Administration (NOAA): 127

National Portrait Gallery, UK: 14

New York Public Library: 43

Pacific Union College: 41, 49

Private Collection (for sale by Southeby's): 15

Reprinted with permission from the *Chronicle Herald*: 85, 116

Royal Botanical Gardens: 13

Sybil Nunn: 7

Tall Ship Bounty Foundation: 103

Tara Boyd: 32, 91

Tell Tale Productions: 122, 124

The Bounty by Jane Alexander: 44

Turner Enterprises: 95

United States Coast Guard: 135, 136, 139, 140, 143, 144, 145, 146

WikiCommons: 89

Wikipedia: 15, 16, 19, 35, 42, 48, 80

Wray Dewar: 72, 74

Index